THE LOOK

Published by Sanctuary Publishing Limited, Sanctuary House, 45-53 Sinclair Road, London W14 0NS, United Kingdom
www.sanctuarypublishing.com

Colour separation by Tenon & Polert Colour Scanning Ltd

Printed in Hong Kong by Midas Printing

Photographs: Courtesy of Malcolm McLaren and Sarah Bolton; with thanks to Hal Lansky and courtesy of The Bernard J Lansky Collection; with thanks to Gordon Millings who supplied material courtesy of Dougie Millings; EMI; Apple Corps; courtesy of Anello & Davide; © Rex Features, London; with thanks to Mario Rebellato at Austin Reed, London; John Stephen; with thanks to Johnny Moke who supplied photos by Robert Holmes, London; with thanks to Colin Woodhead; with thanks to John Simons; © Telegraph/Colorific; with thanks to John Pearse who supplied photographs by Cym Taylor; with thanks to Nigel Waymouth; with thanks to Lloyd Johnson; with thanks to Betsey Johnson, NY, USA; with thanks to Rodney Bingenheimer, LA, USA; with thanks to Kevin Rowland who supplied photographs by Kim Knott and Tim Sullivan; courtesy of Celia Birtwell; with thanks to Antony Price; courtesy of Peter Golding; with thanks to Phil Strongman, London; © NME; © Daily Mirror Archives; with thanks to Jay Strongman; with thanks to Tamsin Tyrwhitt at The Lifestyle Company, London; with thanks to Sheila Rock; with thanks to Boy George and Eileen Schembri; with thanks to Marc Lebon; with thanks to Phil Knott; © Sounds Magazine Archives; Shilland & Co; with thanks to Antony Price; with thanks to Mark Powell; with thanks to Debbie Waite at the Paul Smith office, London; with thanks to Stussy UK; with thanks to Wayne Hemingway; courtesy of Michael Koppelman; with thanks to Max Karie & Pippa Brooks of Shopgirl Inc; with thanks to Olaf Parker and Susan Denney at Burro Studio, London; with thanks to Wendy Hunt at BPI who supplied photographs by JM International; with thanks to Chris Taylor, London; with thanks to Bruce Marcus aka Count Indigo; with thanks to Leslie Gardner; with thanks to Anotella Viero at Diesel, London; with thanks to The Outside Organisation.

Front and back cover photographs
With thanks to Max Karie and Pippa Brooks who supplied the photographs by Libi Pedder

Author photographs
Sainsbury's, Clapham, London

ISBN: 1-86074-302-1

Contents

Foreword
by Malcolm McLaren

We are all aware of fashion. The supermodels of today are among the biggest stars in the world. But they are silent icons, and the mysterious appeal of the beauty industry continues to grow. Fashion is the visual expression of a culture. Paradoxically, it can be both sublimely sophisticated and carnally bestial at once. Fashion is used as a means of sexual display, status symbol and tribal code. This is a story about fashion. Fashion is one of the most elusive subjects, but it is precisely this elusiveness which fascinates. Fashion has an ability to take over people's lives to an astonishing degree. Fashion can never be pinned down; it is constantly morphing into something else. No one completely escapes it. Youth, irreverence and anti-fashion statements are coveted, as they can never be bought, but in various forms they can be taken up and converted into fashion before being discarded. Fashion is as ruthless as it is fickle. The extraordinary hold fashion possesses lies in its ability to provide identity. Everyone who enters this world has a different reason or motive for doing so. Sometimes it is simply the result of a chance encounter, but once they are truly ensconced it is almost impossible to escape.

At the age of 25, I designed one of my first pieces of clothing, a bright blue lamé suit, my first rock 'n' roll suit, which I intended to wear walking down the length of the King's Road. I was looking for one of those chance rendezvous that would change my life. This was 1971, and the King's Road in Chelsea was full of people, a parade of late-'60s fashions and styles, a dropped-out, motley group of hippie emporia - Bazaar, Alkasura, Granny Takes A Trip. I was counting on that unexpected moment of glamour, and I found it at number 430. In this black hole at the end of the King's Road, I changed my life. In the shop's various incarnations - Paradise Garage, Let It Rock, Too Fast To Live Too

Young To Die - I made clothes that looked like ruins. I created something new by destroying the old. This wasn't fashion as a commodity; this was fashion as an idea.

A later incarnation of the shop was called Sex. It had a range of fetish and bondage paraphernalia, mostly all in black. Black expressed the denunciation of the frill. Nihilism. Boredom. Emptiness. How do you dress an army of disaffected youth? I and my partner at the time, Vivienne Westwood, designed our own military trousers and put a strap between the legs, binding one knee to the other, and stitched in a zipper that went straight down the crotch and wound its way up the arse. These trousers, our bondage trousers, were about the explosion of the body, a declaration of war against repression. They were the perfect uniform for people battling against the consumerist fashions of the High Street.

Sex translated into fashion becomes fetish, and fetishism is the very embodiment of youth. Youth has to behave irreverently - it has to take drugs because of its fundamental belief in its own immortality, which it needs to assert over and over again. Fashion and music are the natural expressions of youth's need for confrontation and rebellion, and fetishism in both is its necessary razor's edge, the exhilarating border between life and death. Fashion and music - music and fashion - are the expressions of the same needs. In retrospect, it now seems natural and right that *The Look* should show how shops such as mine and others on the King's Road throughout the '60s and '70s and '80s produced a street fashion which would inevitably act as a catalyst for the musical tastes of the time.

John Pearse, who created Granny Takes A Trip in the '60s, used an American car that appeared as if it had crashed right through his window. His clothes - velvet suits with loon pants - brought back the Regency dandy. There was also Tommy Roberts, who created pop-art

Beale Street, Memphis, spring 1952. In those days, there were crowds everywhere, day and night, promenading in their finery, shopping on the pavement, dipping into bars, restaurants and gambling dens, meeting on the corner. Excluded by Jim Crow laws from the downtown area at night (although many held down essential but menial jobs in that part of the city during the day), the adult black population of Memphis congregated on Beale to sample each and every variety of leisure activity: sex, whiskey and song, and much, much more.

The mandatory stop-off on Beale Street for the style-minded was the Lansky Bros menswear store at number 126, a hive not only for the city's high-rollers and juke-jointers but also for folks from all over the south, particularly plantation workers on rare trips up to town to buy "high fashion" suits or snazzy pairs of shoes to impress their country cousins back home. In keeping with the rest of the trade on the thoroughfare, Bernard and Guy Lansky's custom was almost entirely black, aside from the rare hip white guy who ventured into the neighbourhood to pick up a shirt with a Hi-Boy collar or a pair of those slim-fit mohair pants with no back pocket which accentuated your ass and drove the girls crazy.

Often that spring, there was one particular kid - noticeable for the mass of greased-up dirty-blond hair pomped atop his head - who often lurked outside Lanskys', sometimes gazing longingly at the brash fabrics and colourful garments in the jazzy window display or, if he was feeling adventurous, taking a peek inside at a gambler flush with winnings being fitted for a gaudy tailor-made.

Elvis Presley was just 17 years old at that time, just about to leave Humes High School and working at the Loews Picture Palace on Main Street. When he wasn't at the Loews - and he soon left when he had a punch-up with a fellow usher - he would just hang out in the area, sometimes driving around in the 1941 coupé his parents had bought with an insurance windfall, but mainly heading on foot for the bright-lights, big-city atmosphere engendered by the neon-lit area's juke joints and pavement parade.

When he wasn't at Lanskys', Elvis would make a bee-line for Charlie Hazelgrove's record shack on North Main, where everything was cool. Charlie let kids sit, sip their sodas and take in the sounds while fans, musicians and wannabes mingled. It didn't cost anything, but Elvis could soak up the atmosphere and get just a little taste of what it would be like if he ever made it as a performer.

Lack of money was no big deal at Charlie's, but Lansky Bros was a different matter. Their prices were high. A tailor-made suit would set you back $69.95 - the equivalent of around $2,000 today. With shabby clothes and holes in his shoes, Elvis had no option but to press his nose against the window and stare at the apparel within, until one day his reverie was broken by Bernard Lansky, who stepped outside to chat with the kid. "I seen him a lot of times out there. He stood out in the crowd even then," says Bernard Lansky, now 73 and still running Lansky Bros, housed now within the ritzy confines of Memphis' centrepiece hotel, the Peabody. Since those early days, Beale has bounced back from the effects of the Reagan-era depression, and has been reborn as an anodyne tourist haven replete with themed restaurants and musical heritage museums. "So one day I went out and spoke to him, invited him in," recalls Lansky in his rich southern tones, taking time off in the lobby of the Peabody from the store which, to this day, he opens at 6.30am every morning. He is now the sole owner, having bought out his brother in 1980. "He was just so polite, was Elvis. It was Mr Lansky this, Mr Lansky that. I told him, 'I'm Bernard; my father's Mr Lansky,' but he didn't let up. He said he was an usher at the Loews and had to go on to work, and I said to him, 'Well, when you get time, why don't you come by and see me?' Elvis said, 'I don't have no money now, but whenever I get rich I'm gonna buy you out.' I told him, 'Do me a favour, will you? Don't buy me out, just buy from me.' And that's just what he did." So it came to be that the King-in-waiting was true to his word, and together Presley and the Lanskys helped define '50s rock 'n' roll flamboyance.

To rewind just a little, the Lansky brothers were doing just fine long before Elvis started maintaining his vigil outside the store front at number 126. "We started in 1946, way before Elvis even thought about us," says Bernard. "The blacks had to stay on Beale Street - they couldn't go downtown onto Main - so when they got off work they'd come up here and they'd shop. Beale Street was their own main street."

Bernard's and Guy's father, Samuel Lewis Lansky, came to Memphis in the 1910 from Kiev, in the Ukraine. He ran a grocery store on Kansas and Fays, complete with gas pump, where his entire family, including all six sons and three daughters, worked and gained valuable lessons in retailing. Right after World War II, old man Lansky put up $300 so that his sons - Frank, Guy, Irvin and Bernard Jnr - could buy 126 Beale Street to run as their own outlet.

The property's history before it was Lanskys' speaks volumes about the colourful environment into which the young men launched their new business. "The guy that owned the store was killed in a robbery," recalls Bernard. "They found the two guys that did it holed up in St Louis, by which time my daddy had been and bought it for us. It was laid out like a flea market there, with old ladies' shoes for sale and a big old pot-bellied stove out back. We cleared all that shit out and went into the army surplus business."

Rationing was still in force and traditional clothing materials were in scant supply, and as a result items such as tailored and off-the-peg suits and cotton shirts were scarce and commanded a high price. The Lansky brothers bought up military dead stock and sold cut-rate fatigue pants, army shirts, marine boots, socks and coats. Such clothing became staples in the wardrobes of post-war youth around the Western world; the beats adapted their look to accommodate heavy denims and leather jackets as they travelled America by road. In the UK, throughout the '50s army surplus defined fashionable boho chic. Roll-neck sweaters and seaman's duffel coats became the uniform for impoverished art students, would-be beatniks and fans of trad jazz. In post-war Memphis, however, army surplus was a necessity for poorly-paid workers. "It went really well because we'd charge just 95¢ for a cap, or you could pick up a pair of pants for $1.95," says Bernard Lansky. "We did a helluva job for a couple of years, until supplies started to run low, and when they did we looked

around for something else and decided to go into menswear."

In his introduction to a catalogue accompanying the Archives of Graceland charity auction at the MGM Grand Hotel in Las Vegas in October 1999, Bernard explains, "We had seen a void in the Memphis market. Practically everyone was selling the same old things everyone else was selling. No one was selling really high-fashion clothes. I mean, we carried nothing but the finest. That's what the kids of the late '40s/early '50s wanted, and we gave it to them."

In the '40s, the zoot suit (a tailor-made act of rebellion in itself, displaying a flagrant disregard for whitebread austerity proudly worn in wide lapels, absurdly-high-waisted trousers and "wasteful" expanses of cloth) had set the tone for what Bernard Lansky still calls "high fashion" during the post-war years, particularly among the Latino and black communities of American cities. Indeed, the zoot suit is said to have been invented on Beale Street by a tailor called Lettes.

The zoot ethic was about excess and nothing less: over-long key chains; two-tone co-respondent wingtips; long, sharp shirt collars after the style popularised by trumpeter Billy Eckstine; fat painted ties. The shape of the man's drape-cut suit which had been prevalent throughout the Western world since the early '30s was extended and distorted with highly padded shoulders, tight waists and pants which ballooned clownishly at the knee.

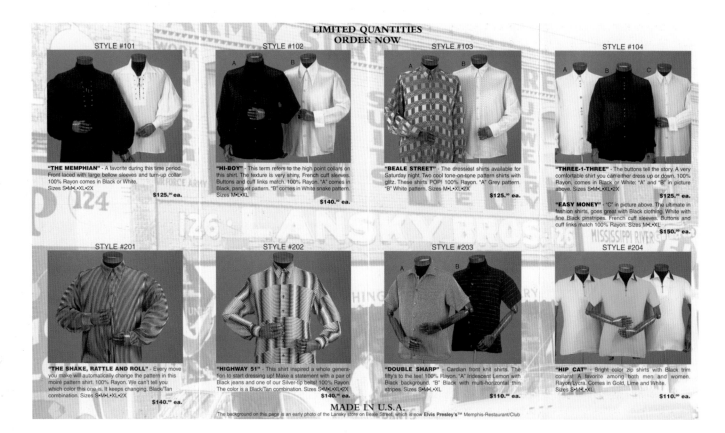

right & opposite
Clothier To The King catalogue, 2001

At the beginning of the '70s, Lanskys' returned to its roots as a black outfitter, launching their Superfly range to match the wave of blaxploitation films and the new funk and soul which filled the airwaves in Memphis. Resident in Las Vegas or Los Angeles for most of the early '70s, Presley's patronage may have dwindled but he never stopped buying from the store, as evinced by the black velvet Oleg Cassini fedora with silver metallic band that he bought at Lanskys' just before Christmas 1972, along with two coats, for a total of $262.50. "He kept with us," says Bernard. "He was a loyal customer. He always came back. You've got a friend, you always come back to see them. A lot of time, he'd call and invite us over to watch movies at his place." But the Lanskys were wise enough to steer clear of the men's-club antics indulged by the Memphis Mafia. "I knew all those twelve guys," says Bernard. "Ain't nobody had a job or nothing. I had a wife and two kids and a business. I was outside looking in and didn't want to be inside looking out."

While he remained loyal to Lanskys' for the rest of his life, Elvis had frequented other shops and designers right from the mid '50s, particularly in Los Angeles, where Parker placed his charge on the Hollywood movie production line for his disastrous run of 22 increasingly kitschy films.

In as far back as June 1956, Elvis began to acquire stage wear for himself, bassist Bill Black and guitarist Scotty Moore from Squire's Clothes in Hollywood when he was in town for live shows. Among the King's most famous outfits is the 24-carat gold lamé suit worn on the cover of the compilation *50 Million Elvis Fans Can't Be Wrong*, issued in March 1960, just as he completed his stint of military service in Bremhaven, Germany. The suit was hyped as having cost $10,000, and was made by Nudie Cohn, Hollywood tailor of custom-made western wear, who started his business after the war supplying costumes for the hundreds of cowboy films being produced at the time. Nudie (real name Nuta Kotlyarenko, a Russian émigré whose colourful past saw him making G-strings and outfits for strippers and prizefighting, although not simultaneously) had made the suit for Elvis in the late '50s, and its appearance on the album cover triggered a switch in Nudie's business to supplying rhinestone- and diamante-encrusted clothing for country and western stars from the massive Nudie's Rodeo Tailors store on Lankershim Boulevard, North Hollywood.

The Nudie suit was but one aspect of Elvis's visual style, which was modified throughout the '60s to accommodate the changes in fashion caused by the new wave of pop following in the wake of the British invasion, although the jet-black quiff – short or long – remained inviolable. In 1968, his rejection of the movie industry and concomitant decision to get back to his musical roots was typified by the clean-lined black leather jeans-style suit worn in the Singer/NBC TV comeback special recorded at Burbank in June that year. That suit was designed by Bill Belew, whose Hollywood-based IC Costume Company provided the King with stage costumes and casual daywear from that point on.

It's interesting to note that much of the clothing supplied by IC harked back to the style created for him by the Lanskys. Look no further than the early-'70s black jacket with red leather pocket flaps and fabric-covered buttons (a Lansky speciality), or the range of jazzily-coloured casual shirts with elasticated cuffs and long, pointed collars. Among the more outrageous outfits that Elvis was sporting by 1974 was a heavyweight wool-blended red coat, lined with red satin and with a black fur collar and detachable cape.

Elvis's final years are marked out in pop history for the disastrous effect that the Vegas treadmill had on his performing talent and his health. The jumpsuits which became the "fatburger" trademark had originally been designed by Belew, and were extraordinary articles of clothing, featuring rhinestones and studding and accompanied by elaborate accessories such as the peacock belt, which was made of white leather with blue-and-gold embroidery and brass discs depicting flying birds.

One of the first jumpsuits, a 1971 item worn for a series of engagements at the Hilton in Sin City, was made from a black, moderate-weight material, lined in satin, with a studded green patent-leather collar and yoke and green vinyl inserts in the pants legs. At that time the jumpsuit had become a fashionable item in music circles, sported by black music contemporaries of Elvis such as James Brown. It would be adapted

above One of Elvis's first jumpsuits, worn for gigs at the Las Vegas Hilton, 1971

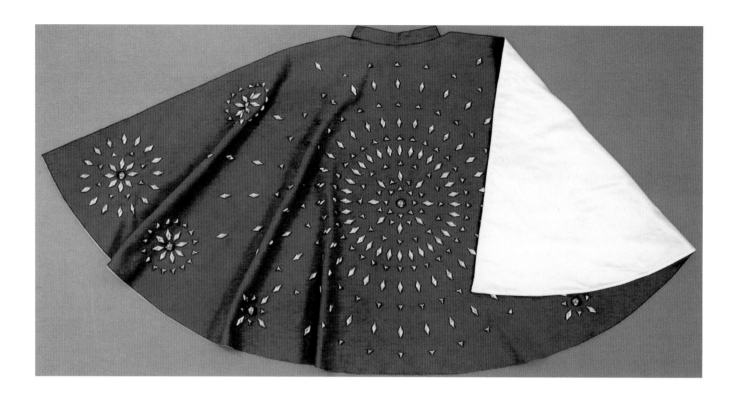

above "Vegas years" cape, designed by Bill Belew

into a slinkier, sleeveless form for Mick Jagger on The Rolling Stones' US tour the following year by British designer Ossie Clark.

Belew's IC Costumes created the extremely camp but enduring Vegas template, while another of the company's early innovations was the cape, in particular the famous light-blue, waist-length version decorated with flat gold studs in a circular pattern. Elvis wore a red version with matching jumpsuit when he performed 'Burning Love' at concerts in Virginia, Arkansas and Texas in the spring of 1972, as featured in the *Elvis On Tour* documentary. The addition of the cape to Elvis's on-stage uniform made the ensemble complete, and soon he was wearing the classic, high-collared, white-rhinestone-studded jumpsuit most associated with his '70s appearances. This was not made by Belew, but was instead created for Elvis by another favoured Hollywood costume-maker, Bob Mackie.

In effect, Belew had updated '50s flash by constructing stagewear which pressed home the changes in Elvis's public persona. On his first night at the Hilton, Elvis dispensed with the country tunes which had been live performance staples. Instead, the show started with an over-wrought rendition of the theme from *2001: A Space Odyssey* and ended with Elvis accompanying himself dramatically on the piano to his version of 'The Impossible Dream'.

All of this is a mighty long way from the skinny kid with holes in his shoes who lurked nervously on Beale Street. Just as time wrought its changes

on Elvis, so it did on Lanskys'. In the mid '70s, the business diversified and launched a chain of a dozen Big & Tall men's clothing stores across the south while Beale took an economic beating, as evocatively detailed in Joni Mitchell's 1977 song 'Furry Sings The Blues': "Pawn shops glitter like gold tooth caps/They chew the last few dollars off old Beale Street's carcass." Hal Lansky concurs: "The Peabody was almost a parking lot in the '70s, and Beale Street looked like a war zone – buildings boarded up and everything gone to rack and ruin."

But not quite. Pulled back from the brink by urban renewal projects and the tourist dollars brought in by the worldwide fascination for the life of Elvis, Memphis is now flourishing, as is Lanskys'. All the while the company concentrated on the Big & Tall trade and the Peabody, it cannily retained ownership of the original Beale site, even after the store closed in 1992. Several offers were made for it, including one from a consortium representing Jerry Lee Lewis, but in 1996 Bernard struck a deal to lease the building to Elvis's ex-wife, Priscilla, and Elvis Presley Enterprises Inc for 20 years for an undisclosed amount. "That was my insurance policy," smiles Bernard.

These days on the block, there are two large windows facing Second Street showcasing vintage Lanskys' clothes, and in the summer of 2000 the Peabody franchise expanded into a fourth unit within the hotel under the name Lanskys': Clothes That Rock. "We're going back into it," says the ever-chipper Bernard. "We know the style, the cut – we know what's happening. We can go right back into it without missing a stroke." At Clothes That Rock, you can find the Clothiers To The King range, based on designs popularised by Elvis, including the Hi-Boy and the Memphian (a front-laced shirt with billowing sleeves selling at $125). Inevitably, there is now also a Lanskys' web site, complete with fan mail, vintage photographs and audio clips of Elvis talking about the store, all available for downloading at www.lanskybros.com.

Bernard Lansky is delighted that his name is now being carried into the digital age, but he prefers to cherish his personal memories of the King in his '50s prime, like the time that he wound up trading a three-wheeled Messerschmitt automobile in exchange for a buying spree at the store. RCA Victor had given the novelty vehicle to their new star when his record sales racked up more than a million copies in 1956. "The first thing he did was come down to the store and say, 'C'mon, let's take a ride.' So we went around the block. When we got back, I said, 'Wait a minute, Elvis. When you're done with this thing, it's mine.' Thirty days later, he called by and gave me the car. He was nice. If he liked you, he'd love you. I stayed out at the house with him when his mother died – got him all dressed up and ready for the funeral. He loved his mom, and he was his mom's only child. After that, everything went to hell in a basket."

3 "Don't Make Us Look Like The Shadows"

The round-collared suits worn by the Fab Four as their popularity exploded in 1963 are the clothes which put Dougie Millings' name on the international map as The Beatles' tailor. Within a year or so of his first encounter with Epstein's charges, Millings played a self-mocking role as a miserable tailor in *A Hard Day's Night* while performers, musicians, aristocrats and foreign dignitaries mingled in line waiting for suit fittings at his small premises in London's West End. The fact that The Beatles were frequent visitors meant that, during school holidays, Millings was inundated with autograph-seeking fans, who laid siege to his premises and necessitated calls to the police to clear the way. However, the turning point in Millings' career had actually occurred five years earlier, on a fateful day when he argued with his employer, the Shaftesbury Avenue menswear pioneer Louis Austin.

Dougie, the Edinburgh-born son of a Customs and Excise officer, had passed his apprenticeship as a cutter in both his home town and also Leeds when he arrived in London in the mid '30s. He cut his teeth working for Hector Powell, the Regent Street flagship store of the men's chain of outfitters', whose promise to customers was to deliver Savile Row quality at suburban prices. In those days, when the average British weekly wage was around £3, a Savile Row suit would have cost in excess of £50, while the mass-market store Burton's charged just £2 10s. Hector Powell suits sold for around £7, and the talented, speedy and hard-working Millings was soon a hit, supplementing his income with night work singing in a band and playing guitar at dance halls such as the Charing Cross Astoria, where he encountered a very different *milieu* from the BBC announcers and West-End businessmen who frequented the Regent Street outlet.

After the war and demobilisation, Dougie started at Austin's, where he carved out a reputation for himself during the '50s as the only cutter on the premises. As a result, the clientèle were often more keen to deal directly with Dougie than with Louis Austin. This inevitably caused tension with the temperamental proprietor. "I got on with Louis quite well," says Millings, "but he was a short man, and very bossy. He'd come in and say, 'I don't want any bloody smoking in the shop,' but he'd be smoking a cigar, blowing it into my face. He had a terrible habit of calling me Millings. I used to think, Christ, this is worse than being in the army. There were four of us, all cramped together. The other two had been there 20 years and were frightened of this little man."

Then, one day in 1958, he snapped, absurdly over a visit to the lavatory. "Louis asked me if I'd been smoking when I got back from the toilet," he laughs. "I told him I'd actually been up there to move my bowels, and thought, 'This is it.' I told him I was leaving a week on Friday. He said, 'How much? It's got to be money, because nobody leaves me.' I told him not for £1,000 a week; not for anything would I stay." Dougie left the shop that night, his bravado dissipating rapidly as he pondered his future. At the corner of Shaftesbury Avenue and Wardour Street, outside the four-storey outfitters' Cecil Gee, he heard somebody call his name. "I looked round and it was Tito Burns," he says.

Burns is the legendary British booking agent and manager who handled the careers of a number of leading acts in the '50s and '60s, such as Dusty Springfield and The Zombies. The power Burns wielded, and his wily negotiating tactics, are laid bare in *Don't Look Back*, DA Pennebaker's landmark fly-on-the-wall documentary about Bob Dylan's 1965 UK tour.

Back in the late '50s, however, Burns was about to play a pivotal role in Dougie Millings' career. "That day, Tito said to me, 'I've got a new boy who's going to be great. Could you make him a suit for Friday?' This was Tuesday. I asked him the name of the new act, and Tito said, 'He's going to be Cliff Richard.'"

Burns only managed Richard for a short spell, but the £25 commission for a white sharkskin suit set Dougie on an immediate hunt for premises to start up on his own. On the day that he was stopped by Burns, another acquaintance told him of a first-floor room available at 63 Old Compton Street, right in the heart of Soho. At that time, this address also housed John Michael Ingram's Sportique. Next door was the Two I's coffee house, named after its original owners, the Irani brothers, who had subsequently sold the lease to Australian wrestlers Ray Hunter and Paul Lincoln. Crucible of the mid-'50s skiffle and homegrown rock 'n' roll explosion, the Two I's was the spawning ground not only for Cliff Richard and The Shadows but also for singers such as Tommy Steele and novelty acts such as the outrageous "Wee" Willie Harris, who sported check suits in clashing tartans and a ludicrous ginger curly hairstyle. It was also a haven for such movers and shakers as manager Larry Parnes – who steered the careers of a host of pre-Beatles stars, including Adam Faith, Vince Eager and Dickie Pride – and songwriter Lionel Bart.

"There's a place for you!" exclaimed Adam Faith excitedly in his 1961 autobiography *Poor Me* (which promised "the truth about the teenage world by one of its biggest stars"). "Nearly everyone who worked at the Two I's has become something in the beat business. One of these days, someone is going to write a musical about that place." This prediction

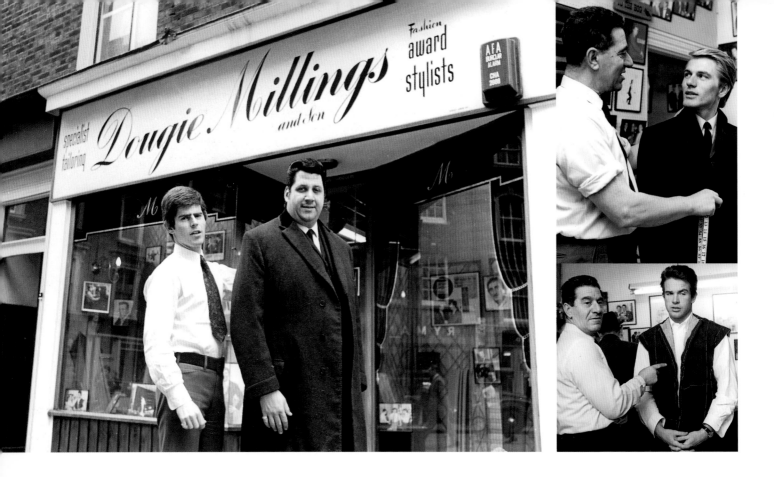

would eventually be realised when the Two I's featured in Julien Temple's flawed 1985 musical movie version of Colin MacInnes' *Absolute Beginners*. Faith (real name Terence Nelhams) goes on to relate how the image-conscious TV producer Jack Good spotted his potential during a shoot at the Two I's for his TV programme *Six-Five Special*. Good decided to turn Faith into "the singing James Dean", and Faith subsequently made his television debut in a black jacket and matching black casual shirt from Austin's.

Thus the siting of the empty premises was extremely appealing to Dougie. "I went straight around there and saw the old lady who owned the building. Here was an angel delivered to me. I told her I had £38 in the bank but a lot of potential customers. She said the rent would be £25 a month, including tea and sandwiches, which she made every day. The woman was angelic."

As he had threatened, Dougie left the employ of Louis Austin a week on Friday, taking with him a lot of custom. "I moved in, and the phone started ringing," he says. "I had a brass plate put on the door. It was very cheeky: "Dougie Millings – Showbusiness Tailor". They all came: Eden Kane, John Leyton, Marty Wilde, Tommy Steele, Adam Faith, Wee Willie Harris. You'd never know. The phone would go, and they'd come flooding in, up the stairs. They would also come from America, like Liberace, Steve McQueen, Warren Beatty, Sammy Davis Jnr, The Four Tops, The Temptations. We even had Buddy Holly when he came over to tour, and

Gene Vincent."

Suits were *de rigueur* for performers in the late '50s and early '60s, and demand was high, so Dougie was soon living up to the "cheeky" title he had inscribed on the shop's nameplate. More than once, larger concerns tried to corral his talents. A couple of years after he opened for business, when Dougie was standing outside the Cecil Gee store, studying the window display, "Cecil Gee himself came out and asked how much would it take to buy my name out. I refused him flat."

Dougie's success was due not only to the quality and speed with which he would deliver but also to the fact that his approachable and familiar style of business emulated the quiet revolution that was already under way in pop in the early '60s, as newcomers swept aside traditional structures. His son Gordon, who trained as a tailor at the up-market Huntsman & Sons before joining his father's company, explains: "If you were to go to the Savile Row firms and order half a dozen suits, the first question would be, 'Who were you recommended by, sir?', and if you weren't they would request you please come back with a couple of recommendations. We operated very differently."

Other showbiz tailors, such as Cyril Castle and Bobby Valentine, were charging around £50, while Savile Row prices at the beginning of the '60s averaged £100. "If you went to Dougie, you got it for £30 in ten days. Didn't have to wait a year, and could have any style you wanted," says Dougie, who worked seven days a week and would often travel to measure

had been in John Lennon's first band, The Quarrymen – pointed out that the silk labels would double the price of the clothing, John Lennon snapped back, "We're not business freaks. We're artists."

With such lack of financial control, the store – which was decorated with a building-high psychedelic mural designed by The Fool – was doomed to failure and closed within seven months, in July 1967, reportedly at a cost of £100,000. In the final few months, Shotton had been replaced by John Lynden, who had a theatrical background and would later stage shows for such artists as Cilla Black. "Lynden was a very nice guy, and he really worked on getting more mainstream gear in, like hipsters and leather jackets," says Bramwell. "It was just about looking likely to make money when the decision was made to shut up shop. I think they just got bored with the hassle, so the doors were opened and they let anyone who came in take what they wanted. Within two days, everything had gone."

After the Apple Boutique closed down, The Fool immediately recorded an eponymous album for Mercury US, whose A&R director heard the result with as much horror as those who had witnessed their clothes designs. "I vomited when the LP was released," he later recalled in *Mojo* magazine. "It was dreadful, and sold about three copies."

Simultaneous to the opening of the boutique, The Beatles also operated Apple Tailoring in the King's Road. Situated next to the Zarathustra nitespot (latterly Wedgies), the shop was run by the late John Crittle, an Australian, who went on to run one of the key Chelsea outlets, Dandy Fashions. With the tailoring department on the ground floor, the basement was occupied by Apple Hairdressers, run by one Leslie Cavendish, who had been poached from leading society crimper Leonard of London. "The boys used to go there quite a bit," says Tony Bramwell. "There's a picture somewhere of George having his hair cut there, while

above Between 1963 and 1967, The Beatles moved from Dougie Millings to the likes of Tommy Nutter

Dougie Millings & Son

(ORIGINAL BEATLES TAILOR) LTD

DOUGIE MILLINGS

right Millings' original designs are now available again

Paul was always wearing one of the pinstripe jackets from Apple Tailoring. John was a very good tailor, and the suits were excellent. He also made some fantastic hats; George wore a great yellow felt number to the *Yellow Submarine* première."

One of the more successful fashion collaborators with The Beatles in the latter half of the '60s was tailor Tommy Nutter, instrumental in Savile Row losing its fusty image by catering to the non-traditional demands of celebrities and pop and movie stars. Nutter helped to re-invent the suit as a hip article of clothing through his work with The Beatles. Dougie first encountered Nutter when he was a messenger with a firm in Mayfair's Burlington Arcade. "This boy Nutter came along one day and said, 'We've got Ringo Starr in the shop. Have you got his pattern, because we'd like to borrow it,'" says Millings, still affronted by the memory. "I said, 'Of course you can't!' But they started using him anyway. Cilla Black – who was also managed by Epstein and was close to The Beatles for a time – backed him, and he was a good frontman. Very talented."

Nutter, who died in the early '90s, employed Edward Sexton as one of his cutters, a man who would later be one of the team of fashion experts who helped train Stella McCartney before she was appointed to head up Chloe. Her father, Paul, was the Beatle who remained closest to Millings, and he returned in 1972 to buy touring costumes for his band Wings. Millings also made the suits worn on the cover of their 1974 album, *Band On The Run*.

Although his association with The Beatles declined as their interest in the underground burgeoned, Dougie's showbusiness reputation was sealed and business continued to boom, with the names of most leading pop acts of the day – from PJ Proby to Jose Feliciano via Bill Haley and The Temptations – featuring in his order books. "There were so many different sides to the business," says Gordon Millings. "When we moved to Marylebone, we would have a lot of custom from nearby Harley Street, from the doctors and specialists who had surgeries there, but at the same time acts like The Four Tops would come to us every autumn, like clockwork, when they toured the UK. In fact, in the late '60s we made them some of the first jumpsuits to be worn by pop stars, an all-in-one piece with a zip down the back and matching jackets."

The size of the business also meant that Dougie found himself in some unusual fitting and measuring circumstances. He once received a call from Tom Jones' manager, Gordon Mills, who wanted to order a tuxedo for the star to wear as he opened a season at the Copacabana in Las Vegas in the late '60s. "The only problem was that he couldn't come to the fitting because he had dates in Britain right up until he flew to the States," says Dougie. "I ended up meeting him at Heathrow, and the only place we could sort it out was in the gents. I'd just got his trousers off when people started coming in and wondering what the hell was going on."

Dougie would soon visit the men's rooms at the airport in this capacity again. "Steve McQueen turned up and told me to get in the cab because he had a plane to catch. On the way, he studied the pattern

bunches and once again I used the gents to measure him!"

Today, Dougie's original designs for The Beatles, along with a selection of '60s suits, are available again via a deal with an Italian manufacturer. Priced at around £300, they are matched with Beatle boots and a range of '60s shirts with tab collars. "We've got four of our designs for the boys and four which wouldn't look out of place at Versace – long jackets with velvet collars," says Dougie, who these days is happy in his retirement. He now writes poems, some of which are written in collaboration with Marty Wilde, who dubs him "the fastest shears in the west". He has amassed 10,000 individual poems over the years, some of which he has self-published, but he is particularly proud of one which he gave to Paul McCartney many years ago and which is now framed and hanging on an office wall at the Beatle's company MPL, in Soho Square, just two minutes' walk from the cramped first-floor shop where they first met nearly three decades ago.

By this time, Carnaby was the busiest street in London, if not the entire British Isles. "The sight was guys with back-combed hair running from one shop to another shop with trousers over their arms," says Lloyd Johnson. "It just exploded with Beatlemania and British invasion."

From new designers to the traditional clothing industry, there was a general recognition that Stephen had created a market which would eventually benefit everybody. "Tourists from all over Europe were pouring into London for cheap weekends," wrote Barbara Hulanicki about 1965 in her book, *From A To Biba*. "They could buy suitcasefuls of clothes for virtually nothing as the exchange rate was so good. London was vibrating with French, Italians, Germans and Swedes, coming to listen to the music, see the shops and gawp at the beautiful girls."

Nik Cohn says that Stephen's revolutionary achievement was to introduce a new concept to post-austerity Britain: clothes as pop. "He had records blaring as loud as they would go, kaleidoscopic window displays, garments hung around the open doorways and spilling out across the pavements, in imitation of St Tropez. Clothes had become an adventure."

Personalities and pop stars were keen to be associated with Stephen. The heavyweight champion boxer Billy Walker modelled for His Clothes in as early as 1962, while a couple of years later David Bowie (then David Jones) even boasted in an interview that he was supplying designs for Stephen. "I think people like Cliff Richard, The Bee Gees and Herman's Hermits wore my clothes best," says Stephen now. "They were very different, and all took different styles from me, but they all looked fantastic."

The fact that he was young and glamorous with a James Dean quiff helped enormously. In an interview Stephen gave for *Town* magazine in late 1967, he appears dressed in a *faux*-Regency gold brocade jacket with rocker hair intact. At the age of 31, he was then running a business which extended to 22 outlets and had interests in the US. With a white alsatian called Prince, a Rolls and a Cadillac, he declared, "The menswear revolution has changed Carnaby Street from a dead place into the fashion centre of the world."

Others, such as the equally pioneering John Michael Ingram, were dismissive: "Carnaby Street takes the fashion ideas from others and then bastardises them," he said. However, Ingram was encountering his own problems; he had spread his net across London with outlets such as Guys and John Michael in Soho, Savile Row and the King's Road. As rumours spread about financial troubles, he said, "Carnaby Street did a good job in commercially spreading the designs, but they made a travesty of them. For example, we brought out pointed shirt collars and they made them go down to the navel. We came out with lilacs and mauves and they picked this up but in the wrong colours."

But Stephen also nurtured one of the most distinctive designers of the day, Michael Fish, credited with creating the kipper tie. "He was assistant to one of our buyers," says Stephen. "That's where he learnt a lot about the business." With backing from Barry Sainsbury of the grocery empire, Fish – who also worked at Turnbull & Asser – opened his own shop in discreet Clifford Street in 1966, where his clothes carried the distinctive tag "Peculiar To Mr Fish", as indeed they were; in the following year, Fish memorably wore a male dress, gold paisley jacket and scarf with knee socks and buckled shoes for a *Queen* spread in which he was photographed with playwright Joe Orton, Twiggy and actress Susannah York. Among his other notable designs was the silk jacket with hippy face painted on the back, as worn by Mick Jagger during The Rolling Stones' visit to Tangiers in 1967, the "dress" worn by The Rolling Stones' singer at the free Hyde Park concert in 1969 and the long male dress worn by David Bowie on the original cover of 1970's *The Man Who Sold The World*.

Many years before this, the knives were already out for Stephen. In *Queen*'s "Society Index" of 1965, his name appears in the "No" column of tailors, along with John Michael, Hawes and Curtis and Blades. Of the companies which received the *Queen* seal of approval, only Dougie Hayward could be described as non-establishment. By that time, the magazine also listed Carnaby Street prominently among its list of "where not to be seen".

Savile Row was responding to the gauntlet thrown down by Carnaby. Turnbull & Asser came up with double-cuff shirts in pale purple slub silk at £10 5s in the summer of 1967, while newcomers such as Allsop, Brindle and Boyle in the King's Road accentuated quality in ready-to-wear suits. In August 1967, founder Simon Boyle – whose Simon Shop was later responsible for the skinny pocketed and short-sleeved Simon shirt – was pronouncing, "We seem to dress anyone, from actors and pop-singers to parsons."

In the winter of 1967, ten years after Stephen opened His Clothes in Beak Street, Carnaby was paved over, with rents estimated to have risen by 1,000% during that decade. It immediately became the full-blown tourist trap from which it has never really recovered. While many of the original players moved, on Stephen went upmarket, a move he had started to make a year earlier with an advertising campaign featuring a model sporting a smart dark jacket with matching paisley tie and handkerchief under the ironic tag line "Portrait Of A Hippy". "He's been seen in Carnaby Street and worse," ran the ad copy. "He actually buys clothes there. From John Stephen. Says not many people know about the more sober side. Keeps talking about jackets and suits, trousers shirts and ties. Quality brand names and superior fabrics. Wool and worsted, cashmere and mohair. Tailored discreetly and cut with flair to John Stephen's discerning design. Says John Stephen suits him well. But he doesn't spread it around. Afraid his wife will find out that John Stephen can offer the same quality to women too."

Stephen points out how his operation helped to export British fashion: "We had shops in the States and in Russia – it was really that big – and the international scene were following us. But then we got all these people imitating what we were doing and, because they manufactured in cheaper materials, it all got given a bad name."

Within a few years, Stephen's pop heyday was over, as was the status of Carnaby Street as a credible fashion centre. Nevertheless, he retains a position as the crucial component in the development of menswear. In Nik

concept to the company is illustrated in the note that he issued to Austin Reed's shareholders soon after Cue opened: "I find it difficult to express this to you in detail but its purpose is to cater to young men who like to dress in more advanced styles than normal...To be frank, I have been quite surprised by the amount of business so far achieved in this small department. It means we have got coming into our Regent Street shop men who we never saw before."

Neat and modern, Cue prices were pegged at around the starting price for clothing sold in the rest of the store, hence a two-piece suit would have been around £25 in 1966. Soon, Cue's kudos was increased by the custom of pop stars such as Jeff Beck and the rest of The Yardbirds, and the shop turned around Austin Reed's business. By the end of the '60s, around half of its 56 outlets housed Cue departments, while Woodhead went on to oversee all men's clothes at the company.

Cue also spurred on other traditional operators: Aquascutum followed with Club 92, Harrods with Way In and even Moss Bros opened One Up at its Covent Garden store. For women, Harvey Nichols had the 31 Shop, which sold cocktail dresses adorned with beads and tiny mirrors. "All the mainstream people jumped on the bandwagon," says Woodhead, "and then the manufacturers were forced to make for this market. It wasn't just the John Stephens and those people having it whipped up in the East End for next to nothing."

Woodhead says that Carnaby Street introduced the idea of using colour in men's fashion, "so we came out of grey". It's a neat summation of the Carnaby effect: everything came out of grey in its wake, and,

top left The Cue shop, 1965: "Young bachelor about town"

above & left Alan Aldridge's glossy advertising campaign for Cue

61

interlocked with music, drugs and youth culture, the fashion business was about to sever its traditional roots forever.

At the other end of the scale, individual shoppers reacted to Carnaby by delving back into the past, while canny retailers recognised the value in buying up antique clothing and reworking it for modern youth. Charity shops and street markets were plundered, as were dealers such as Alfred Kemp – whose slogan was "We Fit Anybody" – and military surplus supplier Laurence Korner, both in Camden Town.

I Was Lord Kitchener's Valet, on the Portobello Road, became the public face of this business, owned by Ian Fisk and run by former mod Robert Orbach. "I sold Jimi Hendrix his famous military coat, the one with all the braiding that he wore so much that it just became part of his image," says Orbach. As the scene blossomed, Lord Kitchener outlets were opened in Soho and Chelsea.

"On Portobello, you could pick up a great double-breasted suit for nothing, maybe a pound," says Johnny Moke. "We'd wear wide ties, big hats, but with other, more contemporary stuff, put it together with something else." The look is exemplified at that time by the surreal act The Bonzo Dog Doo-Dah Band, whom Moke befriended in 1966. Drawing on his aunt's collection of vintage and novelty jazz, Moke lent The Bonzos' lead singer, Viv Stanshall, a lot of the tracks which became staples of their set, including the quaint and hilarious 'Jollity Farm'.

Meanwhile, in Chelsea Antiques Market, the stall run by ex-waiters Adrian Emmerton and Vernon Lambert became a must for the ultra-hip, selling sailors' trousers dyed in a variety of outrageous colours, three-button grandad vests, lace shirts, overhauled demob suits and cavalier jackets in upholstery fabrics. The contribution to youth style made by Emmerton (these days an antique dealer in Northumberland) and Lambert (who died in 1999) cannot be underestimated. With Twiggy as an assistant and custom from the pop elite, they rode the successive fashion waves throughout the mid '60s and not only created the market in second-hand clothing but also stoked the ethnic look by importing Indian silk garments. The fact that many of the girls who worked there were also waitresses at rock club the Speakeasy also helped drum up trade. "Even Yves Saint-Laurent came in to pat our backs," Vernon Lambert – who was the partner of Conde Naste Italy's Anna Piaggi – told Nik Cohn. "He told us, 'Keep up the good work, lads.' That pleased us a lot." By 1970, YSL was featuring '40s chic in its new clothing lines.

There were also two likely characters, Paul Reeves and Pete Sutch, who made clothes for hippies but dressed in full '40s costume, although they retained their long hair. They would drive around town in a hearse full of kaftans and bells, which they sold to a number of outlets.

In Kingly Street, around the corner from Carnaby, Kleptomania stocked hats, Gladstone bags, frock coats, '20s boating blazers and velvet double-breasted jackets. "I used to buy them at markets and from theatrical costumiers and do them up, sell them to Dandy Fashions," says Tommy Roberts, who ran the store with his wife and a partner. "We had

The Who, Ringo Starr, people like that coming in. Then we got all this stuff in a Moss Bros sale – diplomats' dinner jackets with frogging – and it really took off. Ended up selling to people like Liberace, because it made such fantastic stage gear."

The vintage boom reached its peak in the summer of 1967, when the *Sgt Pepper* sleeve featured The Beatles in all their *faux*-military finery. But back at the start of the Victoriana craze, just a couple of years earlier, the keenness of one young vintage clothes fan in London, Sheila Cohen, appeared to have got out of hand, such was the size of her wardrobe. At this point, Cohen's boyfriend, Nigel Waymouth, persuaded her that they should open a shop themselves, if only to sell off some of her clothes.

opposite Colin Woodhead, 1965: "If you lot don't wake up soon you're going out of business"

top Pioneering militarywear at I Was Lord Kitchener's Valet, Portobello Road, 1966

bottom *Town* magazine, December 1967

Success depends a lot, they say, on being in the right place at the right time Carvell on an outstanding example

THE REVOLUTION THAT NRLY FAILED

'Carnaby Street is my creation. In a way I feel about it like the way Michelangelo felt about the beautiful statues he had created.'
JOHN STEPHENS

'Carnaby Street takes the fashion ideas from the very few and then bastardises them and overdoes them so that you're not getting just a nasty thing but an overexaggerated cheap nasty thing.'
JOHN MICHAEL INGRAM

'I think men's clothes are a way of life. They can control your thinking. They can definitely control your social life.'
WARREN GOLD OF LORD JOHN

'Keith Richard in court today was wearing a black four-button Regency-style suit trimmed with black braid. With it he had a high white-necked shirt.'
EVENING NEWS

'You now see the beginning of the end of the old Savile Row.'
LOUIS STANBURY

'The difference between giggled at and being chic is about three seasons.'
EDWARD LLOYD

'I think we're going to go through a very elegant age now.'
TREVOR BEER OF WAY IN

'It's so important for men to have a little black something in the wardrobe today.'
JO BESSER OF WASHINGTON TREMLETT

63

6 "Fucking Weirdos – Who Are These People?"

One Saturday lunchtime in early January 1966, a trio of exotically dressed youths set about erecting a bizarre sign above an equally unusual retail outlet down the wrong end of London's King's Road, the World's End. Struggling with the sign, which spelled out the jokey yet knowing statement "Granny Takes A Trip" in art-deco script, they attracted the attention of the crowds of football fans who were on their way to Stamford Bridge. (Whoever Chelsea were playing that far-off day, they were playing them at home.) The fans hooted and jeered at the sign and the interior of the shop, which was decked out as a psychedelic New Orleans bordello, mixing Aubrey Beardsley reproductions with *fin-de-siècle* opulence amid blow-ups of French postcards of naughty '90s minxes in silk stockings, a Wurlitzer jukebox, a horn gramophone, glass beaded curtains and marbellised wallpaper.

"That morning, as we put up the name, people couldn't believe the sight of this shop," says one of the exotic group, Nigel Waymouth, then a would-be painter, who opened Granny's with his girlfriend, Sheila Cohen, an obsessive collector of vintage clothes, and their friend John Pearse, a disaffected mod who had served a Savile Row apprenticeship before bumming around Spain for a year. "All the football crowd were on their way to the ground, and it was like nothing they'd seen before. We got all these comments: 'Fucking weirdos – who are these people?' Of course, we realised we were the first kids on the block."

That they were. Granny Takes A Trip fused the art, clothes and musical interests – not to mention the recreational drug usage – of this disparate trio and created a new dandified style of dress, one which was in no way allied to the rampant materialism of Carnaby Street but which drew on Victorian frills, Edwardian velvets and satins and ethnic exotica as much as it did on beatnik aesthetics and mod sharpness.

As a reaction to modernism, nostalgia had taken hold among London's *demi monde* at that time, particularly the graphic work of Edmund Dulac, Alfons Mucha and the insane fairy-tale art of Arthur Rackham. However, the biggest influence was that of the decadent Aubrey Beardsley, who was the subject of a huge retrospective at the Victoria and Albert Museum in the summer of 1966 and was already being collected by dealers in art and antiques with acute cultural antennae, such as Christopher Gibbs. Granny's picked up on this nostalgic mood and imbued it with pop-art sensibilities. Thus Cohen, Pearse and Waymouth are responsible in many ways for the look which was soon to be known as (whisper it) hippy.

Not just through their clothes, either. Granny's is a very early example of what would these days be described as a multi-media company, with its founders involved in all manner of pursuits, from ground-breaking psychedelic poster art and fashion modelling to record-sleeve design and club promotion. They even recorded a now highly collectable album themselves, nearly a decade before The Sex Pistols were created out of the scene surrounding McLaren and Westwood's Sex shop, which was to occupy premises just a few doors down from the original site of Granny's.

Granny's even had McLaren and Westwood beat when it came to repeatedly overhauling the image and shopfront of their store. The punk founders made much of the transitions of their shop's name in the '70s, from Let It Rock to Too Young To Live Too Fast To Die to Sex to Seditionaries to World's End. During the mid '60s, Granny's may have retained its name but the façade and clothing ranges were transformed drastically several times, often overnight.

Right from the day that the shop opened, the rock 'n' roll cognoscenti swiftly recognised that something new was happening off the beaten track. "Those first days of Granny's were very surprising," considered the amiable Waymouth amid the clutter of his sunlight-flooded studio in Santa Monica, where he has plied his trade most successfully since 1995. Among his recently completed commissions was a portrait of Mr and Mrs Rupert Murdoch. "One morning, we were sitting cross-legged on the floor, passing a joint around, and these two blokes came in. They looked around and said [adopts Liverpudlian twang], "Well, this is a nice place, isn't it? It's yours, is it?" We looked up, and of course it was John and Paul. They were very sweet and very impressed with the shop. They used to come back all the time."

The Beatles were soon sporting the trademark Granny's shirts (wildly patterned and slim fit, featuring long collars with rounded ends) on the back cover of *Revolver*, which came out in August 1966, while The Rolling Stones followed suit in February 1967 by wearing a selection of Granny's gear on the sleeve of *Between The Buttons*. The Pink Floyd also wore the shop's swirling designs to complement the mind-boggling psychedelia and light shows which became their trademark at the underground club UFO.

It's no surprise that the rock elite took to Granny's with such enthusiasm; Cohen, Pearse and Waymouth were products of the same tightly-knit network of clubs, coffee bars and fads which had spawned '60s pop. And the clothes and environment that they created at Granny's paralleled the changes in music which took place when the drugs started to work and pop turned kaleidoscopic.

above Nigel Waymouth, 1967: "Those first days were surprising"

right John Pearse, 1970: "He was sort of a mod, smart and sharp"

At the beginning of the decade, Waymouth - who was brought up in suburban Stanmore - was a beatnik student at University College. Secretary of London University's Jazz Society (he once blagged his way into Duke Ellington's room at the Dorchester and ended up hanging with the maestro for five days), his abiding passion was yer blues, having come across a Muddy Waters record in an Edgware record shop in his teens: "I'd gone in there to buy Elvis's 'Don't Be Cruel' but saw this LP and thought, 'Anybody with a name like this has to be of interest.' I put it on and it just sent shivers down my spine. I never looked back."

Having taken in the nascent Brit-blues scene nurtured by older musicians such as Alexis Korner and Cyril Davies at Ealing's Railway Hotel (where The Stones were part of a shifting cast of amateurs who filled in at the interval, billed as Little Boy Blue And The Blue Boys), Waymouth was a member of the gang of students and enthusiasts who travelled north to the Manchester Free Trade Hall in 1961 when it hosted a package of the first live appearances in Britain by such pioneering American artists as John Lee Hooker, Victoria Spivey, T-Bone Walker and Sonny Terry And Brownie McGhee. "I was so passionate that I went up to Sonny Terry and asked for his autograph, and then suddenly realised he was blind. But he was cool. He put his hand in his pocket and pulled out a stamp pad and just nonchalantly pressed it on my programme."

Later that night, Waymouth was chatting to harmonica player Shaky Jake. "This young boy comes up and says, 'Can I have a go?', picks up the harmonica and starts blowing. Shaky Jake looks him up and down and goes, 'Hey, you a star, man.' Of course, it was Mick Jagger. Him, Brian and Keith had all gone up in a little Mini Minor. Anybody who was into the music had made the effort to get there and meet our heroes."

The music took a couple of years to cross over, but its popularity was boosted by touring package shows like those witnessed by Waymouth. "I remember seeing The Stones, Bo Diddley and The Everly Brothers at what's now the Hammersmith Odeon and the old Finsbury Park Astoria. Seeing The Animals play 'House Of The Rising Sun' for the first time was amazing."

Waymouth's fascination with the blues soon led to other connections, such as the time he went backstage to meet Sonny Boy Williamson after a concert in Croydon, Surrey, in 1963. "That was the first time I came across Guy Stevens," he says of the fanatical proselytiser for black music, who was then DJ at the Scene club and later featured significantly in the Granny's story. "Guy was really switched on, importing records and playing the latest stuff, some of which was incredibly obscure, even in America. Young white Brits were much more hip about what was going on than our American cousins because of the terrible race divisions in the US. It's not the same now, what with the largest hip-hop market being white suburban kids, but then it was a very different deal. But I didn't even know Guy was at the Scene, because I wasn't a mod; I wasn't in that world."

Which is why Waymouth didn't encounter John Pearse until 1965. Pearse had been very much part of "that world", having been a modernist who frequented the Sunday-night dances at the Lyceum ballroom in the Strand while still attending school in Paddington, northwest London, in 1959. "The Lyceum was a very chic place to go," he says, sitting in the calm of his discreet tailor's shop in Meard Street, Soho. Here customers include newcomers such as singer Robbie Williams, as well as old friends Mick Jagger, Jack Nicholson and Christopher Gibbs. Muted classical music fills the air as Pearse - in deliberate, self-deprecating tones - reflects on the scene which stimulated the interest he has had in clothes "since I came out of the womb". Given the quiet intensity of his presence, it is appropriate that Pearse uses the word "edgy" a lot.

He describes the three-button mohair suits he first saw worn at the Lyceum as "fastidious and edgy; they seemed to go with a Vespa GS and still remain clean. Later, the bluebeat thing came in and we'd go to the Flamingo and the Scene, listen to Guy Stevens play his Sue and Island Records."

Buying button-down shirts at Austin's and "edgy, chiselled" shoes at Regent in Wardour Street, downstairs from the Whisky A Go Go, Pearse decided to learn how to make mohair suits himself by taking up an apprenticeship in Savile Row. "When I left school, I worked in a print shop upstairs from the Marquee as a lithograph artist, but I couldn't stand the noise from the machinery. I walked around Savile Row into Henry Poole, which was actually on Cork Street, and asked for a job. They told me to wait, and as I was sitting there David Niven walked in, looking debonair, to pick up some suits. I thought, 'This is great. I'm going to meet stars.'"

But there was no job for him, and Pearse was sent around the corner to Hawes & Curtis on Dover Street, where he was set to work as an apprentice coat maker. "We were upstairs in the workroom, which was like Fagin's lair. Everyone was very young, and it had quite a good ambience for learning the craft. Those guys were all kind of moddy as well, even though they were making the Duke of Edinburgh's kit or the King of Thailand's stuff. It gave me good grounding for the flamboyance to come, because you knew how to make things."

Pearse's talent blossomed at Hawes & Curtis, as evinced by a letter from his employers to his parents dated 26 October 1961, which he later used as a promotional item for his business in the late '90s, juxtaposed with a confrontational picture of himself, cigar stub in mouth and wearing a ponyskin print shirt. The letter reports that he had made satisfactory progress. "I am sure he will make a first-class tailor, if he continues to show the interest and keenness which he has done so far," wrote Mr EH Watson. Pearse's boyish face also appeared in the 2 June 1962 edition of *Menswear*, when he was chosen to be one of a group of London apprentices to present a golden jubilee "stereophonic radiogram" to one Mr Fred Stanbury.

By 1963, Pearse had set up a neat little sideline making clothes for his friends, and had learned all that Savile Row could offer. Like many a mod, from Rod Stewart to Eric Clapton, continental Europe beckoned, and unlike the latter (who opted for a trip to Greece), but just the same as the former, he went travelling for a year or so in Spain, where he knocked around in then-bohemian Torremolinos, on the Costa Del Sol.

At about the time that Pearse was returning from his Spanish sojourn, Waymouth left university and picked up work as a freelance research writer for medical journals based in offices at 488 King's Road, on the corner of Langton Street. His girlfriend, Sheila Cohen – who was also known as Sheila Troy, and has not been in contact with her former Granny's partners since the mid '70s – was one of a small group of hipsters whose reaction to the Swinging London fashion treadmill was to opt out. "She wouldn't buy new clothes, but was obsessed with Victorian, Edwardian, '20s stuff – anything that was old," says Waymouth. "I'd go with her to the flea markets and to Portobello. Eventually, she bought so many clothes that it started to get out of hand, and one day I suggested we should open a shop and sell them."

Cohen's fascination with vintage clothes coincided with growing drug experimentation indulged in by the couple and their circle of friends. "By that time, we were beginning to flirt with dope, and we'd taken a few trips," says Waymouth. "This was in '64/'65. It was very early. We didn't realise how early it was for people to be doing that sort of thing." Through "two camp chicks dabbling in acid", Cohen and Waymouth met Pearse. "He was a sort of mod, smart and sharp, but he had a visual style all of his own," says Waymouth. "One of these girls that lived around the corner, Barbara, brought him along. We liked him – we all got along very well – so I put it to him that we wanted to open a shop and we were going to call it Granny Takes A Trip.

"I thought the name up one day. We were going to be selling granny clothes, and everyone was talking about tripping, so we thought it was a funny joke. John was very keen on the idea, having trained as a tailor. We were on the dole, but John borrowed a couple of hundred quid from

below *Town* magazine, August 1966

his uncle and Sheila had the clothes, I had the design for the shop, so we were off."

Waymouth had already earmarked premises: the ground floor of the offices at which he had worked as a freelance writer. At a rent of £14 a week, the trio set up shop just before Christmas 1965, two months ahead of the coming psychedelic boom marked by the opening of the Indica art gallery and bookshop by book dealer Barry Miles, art dealer John Dunbar (Marianne Faithfull's first husband) and Peter Asher, once of pop duo Peter And Gordon and brother of Jane Asher, whose boyfriend, Paul McCartney, was one of Indica's investors. Indica (the place where John Lennon first met Yoko Ono, at a private showing of her exhibition Unfinished Paintings And Objects, in November 1966) was situated originally in Mason's Yard, Mayfair, which also housed the ultra-hip Scotch of St James.

The choice of location for Granny Takes A Trip could not have been more out of the way. Around the bend of World's End, it was not only across town from the happening areas of Carnaby Street and the West End but it was also a good mile west of the King's Road epicentre, where Mary Quant's Bazaar had established the Chelsea look half a dozen years earlier. One of the few outlets to have already sprung up in the immediate area was Alice Pollock's Quorum, which later moved to Radnor Walk in 1966.

Pearse, always the more urban member of the trio, describes the immediate area as "a complete khazi", and recalls the time he brought along a couple of Savile Row friends to test their willingness to become involved in the venture. "I was the tailoring boffin, and my two partners wanted me to work with them because of my experience. I got some of my tailoring buddies to come down and show them what we were going to do, but they kind of walked away from it because they thought the location was crap, and thought we didn't have a chance in hell down there."

Although Waymouth acknowledges that the situation of the shop doubled the risk, since the clothes flew in the face of the prevailing fashion, he says that Chelsea was a "sympathetic" neighbourhood, given the existence of haunts such as the Pheasantry, the Six Bells and the Chelsea Potter. "Chelsea was always hip because of the artistic connection. People liked it. The King's Road was...er...groovy, man. This wasn't alien territory; it was somewhere really to be considered."

The shop opened with Cohen's vintage clothes supplemented by a small range of Pearse's shirts. Satin ties cost 30 shillings while floral shirts were six guineas, as were white Venetian cloth flares, while second-hand satin blouses were £3 10s. *Town* magazine was mocking yet impressed: "A purple-painted shop stuffed with second-hand clothes for men and women and Victoriana which must have raised a titter when it was new." The vintage stock soon ran down as word got around, and it was replaced with new designs for both men and women by Pearse and Cohen. Shirts and jackets in the ubiquitous William Morris prints were complemented by tight but flared trousers in velvet and brocade, while Cohen supplied velvet and lace skirts, blouses and dresses.

Multi-coloured, full-length suede coats were worn by such

left Interest in *fin-de-siècle* art
blossomed in fashionable circles in 1966

above Hung On You: "Wild, druggy reputation"

customers as John Paul Getty, while in her 1994 autobiography artist Henrietta Moraes recalled a pair of Granny's boots "made in the most fetching William Morris prints, chrysanthemum and honeysuckle. They laced up to the knee and, depending on how stoned I was, took at least ten minutes to put on." A popular later range at Granny's were the patterned shoes from Gohil, the north London-based company which provided high-heeled, multi-coloured leather boots and shoes inset with stars and other designs.

The shop interior itself underwent many stylistic changes but was never well lit - a boon to the dope-smoking owners and clientèle - and boomed out loud music either from the jukebox or the in-store hi-fi. Many visitors found it intimidating and the staff off-hand. "They were always up their own arses at Granny's," says one customer, who declines to be named three decades later. "Always a bit too trendy for their own good."

"The first people to sniff it out were a mixture of Chelsea gays and debutantes," says Waymouth. "Then pop stars started coming pretty quickly after them. We had all these personalities coming through, to namedrop a few thousand, and groups like The Animals would have their photos taken outside." The relatively high price of the shirts (five guineas) did little to deter interest. "They flew off the shelves," Waymouth says ruefully, shaking his head at "the good little scam" of charging in guineas - a shilling (5p) was added to a pound on luxury items such as clothing right up until decimalisation in 1971.

Pearse concurs: "It was completely liberating because you were your own boss, printing money at the age of 19. We very quickly moved into our own creations, with lots of those floral shirts with long collars. It wasn't only The Stones and The Beatles but everybody – The Who, The Small Faces, The Byrds. We knew when the plane had landed from San Francisco."

In the latter act's case, Gram Parsons – who was briefly a Byrds member and attached himself to the London scene after their visit there in 1967 – became fascinated by Granny's. "He used to sleep on the floor of the shop because he liked it so much," says Waymouth. Parsons was particularly keen on a range of jackets inspired by one worn by James Dean's character Jet Rink in the 1955 movie *Giant*. "It had a box back with 'jet' pockets – those curved ones with the darts at the end. It was typical western wear, but John brought something new to it because he tailored it with a bit of London, of Savile Row. We had them with a velvet collar, and they became more elaborate when we added beading." The jackets were made by traditional tailors, such as Foster Bros of Kings Cross, a connection of Pearse's from his apprenticeship days. But Pearse was keen that the shop ventured into pastures new: "We were the first bisexual shop, if you like," he smirks. "We had women's clothes big-time, frocks and blouses, and there was no hard sell because everyone knew everyone else."

Early publicity came via a *Vogue* fashion spread featuring Faye Dunaway modelling Granny's clothes, while the shop also took part in on-air fashion competitions screened by TV pop show *Ready, Steady, Go!*. Among other early clients were The Band, Barbra Streisand and the Andy Warhol/Factory crowd, who dropped in during a visit to London in 1966. Another regular was Brigitte Bardot's sister Mijanou, who bought items for her Paris boutique. "She used to come all the time, sometimes with her gorgeous sister, and all us boys thought our dreams had come true," says Waymouth.

Within four months of opening its doors, Granny's was featured in *Time* magazine's cover story on "London: The Swinging City". The store had rapidly established itself as one of the "boy's boutiques" to drop into in April 1966, along with Top Gear and the original Hung On You, and in doing so had sealed the reputation of the King's Road as being the new place to be seen.

The Times carried a feature entitled "The King's Road Boys", about those venturing west of Sloane Square. "I remember it well," says Lloyd Johnson, "because it featured two of my friends from Hastings, Pat Cockell – my first partner – and Sebastian Keep. They basically got fed up with Carnaby Street and started buying loads of stuff from Granny's. I was working at the Cue shop at the time, and Patrick and I started up our own sideline. I made ties out of strange materials – curtains, whatever – and while I was at work, Patrick would go across to Granny's to sell them."

Dandy aesthete and intimate of the rock elite Christopher Gibbs recalls the trendification of Chelsea, spurred on by the opening of Granny's: "I remember in about 1966 walking down the King's Road with a girl I knew, and most people were dressed in suits or jacket and trousers if they were men and the girls were wearing nice frocks or trousers and jacket. Very occasionally, there would suddenly be someone unusually and noticeably dressed, like a work of art. Plainly a lot of thought had gone into it. And she said, 'You know, we know all these people.'"

Within a year, the transformation was complete. "You'd walk down and everybody would be dressed like that," says Gibbs. "Everything had changed; it had all completely taken over. Everyone started dressing like Gram Parsons or Mick Jagger. It actually became quite difficult to suss out who was a pop star and who wasn't."

Within a year of Granny's opening, Hung On You had been installed by owner Michael Rainey into number 430 King's Road, a few doors down and the most significant address in the story of pop fashion. (It later housed Mr Freedom, Paradise Garage and eventually Let It Rock.) Rainey had worked with Ossie Clark and Alice Pollock at Quorum, and was very much part of the new clothing establishment (his wife was Jane Ormsby-Gore, daughter of Lord Harlech and sister of the dandy Julian, another English Boy model). Hung On You was initially at Chelsea Green, in Knightsbridge, at a site now occupied by the tea shop owned by Paul McCartney's former girlfriend Jane Asher. The up-market area in which the shop was originally situated was very trendy but lacked the creditability supplied by World's End. Nearby in posh Beauchamp Place there was a shop called Deborah & Claire, which sold flowery, puffy-sleeved shirts with long cuffs to the likes of Cream.

At his Chelsea Green store, Rainey reworked vintage clothing: tapered guardsman's trousers with a red stripe down the side, relined dragoon coats and military bandsman's jackets. As well as Liberty-print, mandarin-collar shirts, complete with frills, Rainey overhauled '40s suits to coincide with the revival of the opening of the movie *Bonnie And Clyde*.

Hung On You had a wild and druggy reputation. In the basement, Rainey would thrash around a drumkit, dressed like a member of The Byrds with a Brian Jones haircut and oblong-shaped dark glasses. Customers were handed smiles on sticks when they visited the store.

The move to the King's Road saw a change to all-out hippy, with Kaftans and ethnic garments. Here the assistants, Jay and Bo, would sit on a chaise longue in the window and smoke joints, climbing down to serve customers when duty called.

Artist Henrietta Moraes recalled in her biography how she became "a complete hippy" by frequenting Hung On You and buying the shop's Afghan robes and "edible-looking, ice-cream-coloured suits – white, pink, pistachio-green and cream", while *Town* magazine wrote that Hung On You's clothes were "simple and uncluttered and proprietor Michael Rainey puts a lot of emphasis on colour". He told the magazine in 1966, "We're not tailors but we will make things up for people if we think their ideas are good." Hung On You's suits, with wide lapels and two-button jackets, sold for 35 guineas, while shirts in silver, wine, gold, pink and red satin sold for six and a half guineas apiece.

The Granny's effect could soon be detected in other outlets. By halfway through 1967, Take Six - the chain founded on the back of the Carnaby boom - was knocking out facsimile Granny's velour double-breasted jackets and velvet Regency frock coats for 14 guineas. Meanwhile, Michael's Man Boutique opened its seventh outlet at 122a King's Road and owner Leslie Frankel said, "Carnaby Street is on the wane. King's Road is international. 50 per cent of my customers are from abroad."

Dandy Fashions, which was slightly more straight, was owned by the late John Crittle, an Australian, whose involvement in the London fashion scene had included operating the original Dandy outlet in Baker Street before taking on Apple Tailoring in the King's Road for The Beatles. The father of world-renowned ballet dancer Darcy Bussell, Crittle later returned to Australia, where he died in the spring of 2000.

As a 1966 article in *The Daily Mail* points out, while Quorum was selling a "ton-up" zippered black leather jacket, studded across bust and back, at 15 guineas, Granny's was charging 23 guineas for a heavily patterned "men's art-nouveau jacket in yellow and brown", with the matching cotton mandarin collar shirt with pop-on frill, at four guineas. These jackets were probably modelled most effectively by the now-forgotten pop-psych act Toby Twirl on the sleeve of their Deram single 'Movin' In'.

The *Daily Mail* piece, which describes Granny's as "London's most exotic hippy shop", also details the shop front, which by that time had changed drastically from the opulent mood of the shop's opening: "The facade is covered by the dour face of a Red Indian with red and yellow stripes radiating from his head. Inside: Indian shirts, flowered jackets and wild Jimi Hendrix heads of hair. [Both Waymouth and Pearse sported curly white-man's afros, a look promoted by customers such as Eric Clapton and all of the members of The Experience at the time.] There are the most beautiful shirts of flowered cotton at prices from five guineas and exclusive coats and jackets in floral prints. The Beatles, Stones and Cream come in search of fantasy in their clothes and find it in two rooms, one covered in yellow paint, including the telephone."

Granny's had switched from *fin-de-siècle* revivalism to employing the giant, blown-up photographic portraits of fierce-looking native American chiefs (first Low Dog and then Kicking Bear) for no better reason than "they represented everything that we as hippies - or whatever you like to label us - looked for," according to Waymouth. "They were colourful and sympathetic to us." As *Nova* noted in April 1967, in a photo feature on Granny's and Hung On You, "Warning. By the time this issue is on sale the appearance of these things may well have changed to yet another new design..."

Waymouth says that the drastic image changes were instituted mainly through boredom, "but it was also a good idea to keep changing, like fashion itself. Keep it moving. We used to conceive of something and then design it and usually stay up all night redoing the front so that the next day people would come by and just go, 'Good Lord, what's happened?'"

The most notorious Granny's façade was the pop-art portrait of Jean Harlow that covered the entire front of the shop. Painted by Waymouth and Michael Mayhew, the only means of seeing inside the shop was

through the movie star's mouth. "Sometimes you'd see people looking in, and they'd look as if they were the tongue," laughs Waymouth. "And this was ten years before Malcolm McLaren's shop, which had that same vibe, where people were either terrified of the place or they really felt like coming in and hanging out."

Most ingenious was the decision to bolt the front half of a 1947 Dodge onto the front window in 1968. "It was John's car, and the big end went one day on the way to the airport, but we didn't want to take it to the breaker's yard because it was such a nice thing," says Waymouth, "so I suggested we cut it in half and have the front half protruding from the shop, and as we had the forecourt we could do it."

Granny's reputation ensured that it was raided regularly. "Funnily enough, we were never busted," muses Waymouth. "They thought they could get us, but eventually I think they just used to come round for their own amusement. We were so naïve, we didn't give them backhanders. The mainman at Chelsea Police Station was - can you believe it? - Sergeant Roach. He was eventually thrown out for corruption."

For six months in 1967, the basement of Granny's was occupied by Johnny Moke, who had got to know Waymouth and co because they frequented the same shirt-maker, a Mrs Trotter in south London, who realised the daring designs concocted for sale at the shop. In the basement, Moke sold antique clothes, mainly women's: "We used to cut up blouses and dresses and turn them into shirts or tops for men. What was great about Granny's was that there were no boundaries. Anything went, and they kept on changing. The best clothes they made were the green velvet jackets with red collars - fantastic for the time."

Above the shop lived Judy Scutt, who had worked with Waymouth at the medical research office and made ties and other clothes for Granny's. Her son Paul was then a student at Cambridge, and he occasionally dropped by with his group of friends, who included Jonathan Meades (broadcaster, novelist and future restaurant critic for *The Times* and assistant editor of *Tatler*) and Salman Rushdie (future writer and *fatwa* victim). Meades was not at all enamoured of the Granny's crowd, as he told Jonathon Green in his superb oral history of the English underground, *Days In The Life*: "It was the first time I realised this extreme snobbery based on clothes. I remember Nigel Waymouth sneering at me - you could hardly see his face through this mass of afro hair and this huge collar. He obviously thought I was a jerk and wanted me moved out of the way, because I was an extremely bad advertisement for his shop."

Waymouth doesn't actually remember this encounter ("he obviously thinks I snubbed him; that's his problem"), but eagerly recounts a story about Rushdie which the writer himself recalled for *The Guardian* in January 1995, and one which underlines the hipper-than-thou aura surrounding Granny's. In the piece, Rushdie set the scene by evoking the shop's gloomy interior: "It was pitch dark. You went in through a heavy bead curtain and were instantly blinded. The air was heavy with incense and patchouli oil and also with the aromas of what the police called Certain Substances. Psychedelic music, big on feedback, terrorised your

eardrums. After a time you became aware of a low purple glow, in which you could make out a few motionless shapes. These were probably clothes, probably for sale. You didn't like to ask. Granny's was a pretty scary place."

Although Rushdie mistakenly refers to Sheila as Sylvia (just as he misidentifies Jean Harlow for Marilyn Monroe and the Dodge for a Mack truck), he goes on to sum up her individual style, which pre-dated goth by decades: "She was pale, probably because she spent her life sitting in the dark. Her lips were always black. She wore mini-dresses in black velvet or see-through white muslin: her vampire and dead-baby looks. She stood knock-kneed and pigeon-toed, after the fashion of the period, her feet forming a tiny ferocious T. She wore immense silver knuckle-duster rings and a black flower in her hair. Half love-child, half zombie, she was an awe-inspiring sign of the times."

Waymouth encountered Rushdie a few years back at a lunch given by a mutual friend. "He told me that he sometimes used to stay upstairs," says Waymouth, "and one night this Rolls Royce with blacked-out windows pulled up and out came John Lennon. Salman decided this was the best time to introduce himself and knocked on the partition door. Sheila opened it, huge joint in hand. He said, 'Hello, my name's Salman Rushdie and I thought it was time I introduced myself.' She said, 'Don't you know conversation's dead, man?!', and then promptly shut the door on him. It was typical of that kind of dreadful attitude."

Granny's peaked in around 1967/8, with its profile boosted by involvement in a host of extramural activities. Pearse had already received media attention via his relationship with the beautiful raven-haired model Gala Mitchell, who starred in *Blow-Up*, and he then became one of the founding models for aristocrat Mark Palmer's agency, English Boy. Based in premises behind Quorum, English Boy was launched in February 1967 with a mission "to change the image of British manhood and put the boy, as opposed to the girl, on the magazine cover in the future", according to Palmer, then 24 years old and a fifth baronet.

Pointing out that the models "work during the day in boutiques, art schools or films", *The Daily Mail* displayed the line-up of long-haired dandies under the banner headline "British Manhood, 1967. For years the image of the Englishman was fixed in the minds of foreigners: long-limbed, ruddy-faced, Empire-ruling, stolid, *safe*...but in a changing world the pattern changes."

English Boy's roster included ten women, as well as babies and dogs. Brian Jones and his girlfriend Anita Pallenberg were signed early on, although they never appeared in a fashion shoot, for which their rate was 100 guineas an hour. Mick Jagger and Marianne Faithfull also signed up, as did Christine Keeler and Brian Jones' ex, Suki Poitier.

At around the time that Pearse joined the English Boy roster, Waymouth had hooked up with artist Michael English to form a psychedelic graphic design venture with the suitably trippy name Hapshash And The Coloured Coat. English was the hippy designer *du jour*,

having worked on the first issues of Barry Miles' underground newspaper *International Times*, and also produced early posters for the UFO club in Tottenham Court Road, opened by the scene's leading players, John "Hoppy" Hopkins and Joe Boyd. "I think they wanted a distinctive style," says Waymouth. "The idea was to pair us off and see what happened."

Although Waymouth was not a trained artist, he complemented English extremely well, and over a year and a half the pair produced posters for UFO and the other main club of the era, Middle Earth, as well as record sleeves (for The Purple Gang's appropriately-named album *Granny Takes A Trip*) and promotional work (examples include The Who's single 'I Can See For Miles' and 'What's That Sound?' by the pre-Spooky Tooth band Art).

Wherever there was a major event in the summer of love there was Hapshash, who even provided posters for Jimi Hendrix's series of dates at the Fillmore West in San Francisco that June. One of the rarest Hapshash items is their design for the jacket of Corgi Books' volume of *The New Love Poetry*, which combined dreamy eroticism with art-deco flourishes.

The pair retained an innovatory edge throughout their 18-month collaboration. In the case of the landmark 14-Hour Technicolour Dream held at Alexandra Palace on 29 April 1967, they changed the ink colours for the posters so that there were a huge number of variants within the one print run, as noted by Ted Owen and Denise Dickson's history of the psychedelic poster, *High Art*, which points out that Hapshash "designed some of the most dazzling, beautiful and original psychedelic posters, as good as anything produced in San Francisco, LA or Detroit."

Then one day, regular customer Guy Stevens came into the store and pitched an idea. By now he was head of A&R at Island Records and wanted to make a record to complement the clothes, designs and ideas streaming out of Granny's. The maniacal Stevens, who was later to create Mott The Hoople and produce The Clash's *London Calling*, was at that time one of hippy London's kingpins. He supplied Island act Spooky Tooth to provide backing tracks at Marble Arch Studios, while Pearse and Waymouth improvised over the top as Hapshash And The Coloured Coat. "We were discovered to make music years before The Sex Pistols," says Pearse proudly. "Guy said we could do whatever we wanted over the top while others came along to the sessions, like Amanda Lear and Brian Jones, who played piano, harmonica and guitar." Housed in a Waymouth-designed sleeve and pressed on red vinyl, the Hapshash album is – to contemporary ears, at least – an unlistenable hodge-podge, with one side featuring a single track of chanting overlaid with various sounds, including Pearse scratching away in an untutored fashion at an amplified violin.

The album proved to be a project too far for the Granny's crowd, particularly when it was decided to take the "concept" on the road. "The music sort of interfered," admits Waymouth. "We went off to Amsterdam, trying to recreate this concept album live, which was an impossibility. There were these other characters trying to get in and turn it into a proper pop group, so egos started to clash." This in turn jeopardised the central relationships at the shop, particularly since their business

7 "The Switched-On Look"

Although the Swinging London look exploded across America in the mid '60s, there had been pockets of stylistic development to parallel those in Britain for many years prior to this, particularly in the hipper urban areas of New York, Los Angeles and San Francisco. However, the regional variations were huge, and indicative of the atmosphere in which they blossomed; while New York fashion accentuated edginess and stripped-down cool, the LA look is best exemplified by the dressy *Riot On Sunset Strip* gear as sported by numerous garage bands and the likes of Sonny And Cher. Meanwhile, in San Francisco, a hippy twist was added to match the psychedelic pioneering and gutsy charms of bands from The Grateful Dead to Janis Joplin and Big Brother And The Holding Company.

New York led the way, however. In as early as 1961 and 1962, boutiques such as Etcetera and Chiaro Ascuro opened in Greenwich Village, selling flat Greek sandals and short shift dresses. "Or there were the Little Louis heels, which were very Audrey Hepburn," says Richard Channing, then at the Ivy League store Paul Stuart. "My wife and I would walk around the Village and we'd see girls wearing these shifts which were taken out of Givenchy, hung short above the knee. When we went back to Britain, everyone was raving about the mini, but we'd already seen that. It had become part of summer leisurewear in New York. Obviously, it suited the climate there at that time of year."

In his memoir *Popism*, Andy Warhol recalled the New York look of 1962: "It was a great summer. The folk-singer look was in – the young girls with the bangs were wearing shifts and sandals and burlapy things." The Warhol set were also swayed by their acquaintance with the expat British art director of *Vogue*, Nicky Haslam, who hipped them to what was happening across the Atlantic. "Nicky may actually have started the frilly men's look," gushes Warhol, "because I remember him getting curtain lace at Bloomingdales and tucking it up his sleeves, and everybody would be asking him where he got this 'great shirt' because they'd never seen anything like it. He made us aware of the new men's fashions – the short Italian jackets and the pointed shoes, winkle-pickers – and of the way cockneys were now mingling with the upper classes and things were getting all mixed in and wild and fun."

Warhol experienced this at first hand in a spring 1963 encounter with David Bailey and Mick Jagger, who were staying at Haslam's apartment on East 19th Street. "They each had a distinctive way of dressing – Bailey all in black and Mick in light-coloured unlined suits with very tight hip trousers and striped T-shirts, just regular Carnaby Street sports clothes,

nothing expensive. And of course they were both wearing boots by Anello & Davide." By the following year, however, "everything went young. The kids were throwing out their preppy outfits and the dress-up clothes that made them look like their mothers and fathers, and suddenly everything was reversed – the mothers and fathers were trying to look like the kids."

Both The Beatles and The Stones undertook their first US tours in 1964, and a mod vs rockers theme party was held in honour of the latter band at photographer Jerry Schatzberg's studio on Park Avenue South in October. The party also celebrated the 24th birthday of Warhol acolyte and socialite model Baby-Jane Holzer, named girl of the year by Tom Wolfe in his piece of New Journalism reportage on the event: "Her style of life has created her fame – rock 'n' roll, underground movies, decaying lofts, models, photographers, Living Pop Art, the twist, the frug, the mashed potatoes, stretch pants, pre-Raphaelite hair, *Le Style Camp*."

Holzer exemplified the "switched-on look", which was also promulgated by the youthquake promotion of young British clothing in New York that year, featuring the likes of Mary Quant and Tuffin and Foale. One of the people behind this, UK retailer Paul Young, decided that the best way to translate Swinging London was to open his own shop in Manhattan, which he named Paraphernalia.

With the backing of the large company Puritan Fashions, Young set about recruiting local talent for his store, at Madison and 67th Street, and fortuitously encountered 21-year-old Betsey Johnson, who had worked at *Mademoiselle* that summer after winning a magazine competition which offered a trip to London. "That was it for me," she told *Scene* magazine. "Biba, Mary Quant – it was so inspiring. London told me to be a fashion designer. I can cut and sew wildly, but it never occurred to me to go into this business." Young had been attracted by a Johnson design for a T-shirt. "It was the era of the tight, high armhole, and we all thought it was terrific," said *Mademoiselle* fashion editor Edith Raymond Locke. "We ran a little thing about it in our shopping column and she got orders. Then Paul Young called and said he needed a young with-it designer for his new company."

Johnson visited the store with a suitcase full of clothes. "It was very Englandy," she says. "For a long time, people actually thought I was English." Young promptly launched the Betsey Johnson For Paraphernalia label while she also designed Youthquake fashions for Puritan (which has more recently been associated with Calvin Klein). The Paraphernalia shop itself was created in chrome and glass, with rock 'n' roll blasting and go-go dancers, and soon became the haunt of the *beau monde*, from European

opposite Nineties models wear original '60s designs by Betsey Johnson

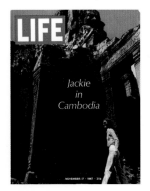

aristos and the Kennedys to the model Veruschka.

Johnson's installation at Paraphernalia provided the new business with some much-needed impetus, and within a year the store was adopting such unique sales techniques as staying open very late, sometimes until 2am. "You'd go and try on things and 'Get Off My Cloud' would be playing – and you'd be buying the clothes in the same atmosphere you'd probably be wearing them in," said Warhol with his usual percipience. "The salespeople in the little boutiques were always so hip and relaxed as if the stores were just another room in their apartment – they'd sit around, read magazines, watch TV, smoke dope."

An art major from Lou Reed's alma mater, Syracuse University, and a resident of the Chelsea Hotel, Johnson had strong ties with the Warhol camp; her fitting model for five years was the fated and epicene Warhol superstar Edie Sedgwick, whom she had met when designing clothes for the Factory movie *Ciao Manhattan*. In May 1967, she encountered The Velvet Underground's viola player, John Cale, at a Paraphernalia fashion show while dating the band's guitarist, Sterling Morrison. "She was doing in fashion what we were doing in music," Cale recalled in his autobiography, *What's The Welsh For Zen?* "It seemed to me she knew everybody I knew...It was a match made in heaven."

Johnson was soon making clothes for the band: a velvet suit for Cale, green and maroon velvet designs decorated with nail-head studs for Morrison and drummer Mo Tucker and a grey suede suit for Lou Reed. "With Lou's suit, everything was fine except for the crotch, which was incredibly exaggerated, so that Lou had this enormous sagging basket he could not fill," wrote Cale. "This did not endear Betsey to Lou. In fact, after that he went out of his way to be rude to her."

Such was the combination of the band's notoriety and Johnson's newsworthiness that an offer to pay for Cale and Johnson's 1968 wedding celebrations came from an unexpected source, she claimed to Victor Bockris in his VU biography *Uptight*. "The awful thing was *The Ladies' Home Journal*, 'The Magazine Of Togetherness', was very much interested in us freaks then," says Johnson. "I must have established some kind of something for myself at Paraphernalia; the press was really great." In the event, the drug-prone Cale contracted hepatitis and the wedding was delayed by four months, by which time the fashion magazine had lost interest. The relationship also added tension to the band's dynamic: "Lou was not very happy [that] John was getting married, period – to me, period," she said in *Uptight*. "It was like the girl breaking up the group."

Cale and Johnson occupied a 1,500-foot-square loft space on La Guardia Place decorated as a battleship, but their "divergent career paths" (Cale's phrase) placed stress on their relationship when Cale left the band to embark on a hefty workload of production, arranging and session chores for the likes of The Stooges, Nico, Nick Drake and Jonathan Richman. He and Johnson divorced in 1971.

Naturally, Johnson was an habitué of the New York underground's premier hangout, Max's Kansas City. This bar/restaurant performed the same function for street designers as the Speakeasy in London, allowing

them to showcase new designs to their target audience. Among other fashion movers and shakers who frequented Max's were womenswear specialists Barbara Hodes and Annie Flanders, YSL designer Maxime de la Falaise, the iconoclast Rudi Gernreich and *Harper's Bazaar* photographer Bill Solano. In 1970, Italian *Vogue* ran a Warhol-style photo spread entitled "Il Mondo Di Max's Kansas City". "I used to have my business people meet me there at Max's cocktail hour, which was really a riot," Johnson says in the 1999 book about the venue, *High On Rebellion*. "It seemed really natural that if they wanted to meet me they should come to my environment. The fashion industry didn't like it. They read it as 'youth', and they weren't young."

Fashion swirled around Warhol and The Velvets. A favourite designer of the Factory crowd and Johnson was Rudi Gernreich, whose fetishistic approach to beach- and leisurewear proved a hit with the New York underground – in 1965, Edie Sedgwick wore a pink lurex Gernreich floor-length T-shirt dress to a film première in Toronto. There were other fashion connections: the glacial vocalist Nico was often teased by her cohorts for

above Jackie wears Betsey

right Betsey Johnson's pre-punk '70s work

a name for herself with a dress made out of electric lights and another with the word "Love" inscribed on the front and "Hate" on the back – operated Kaleidoscope on East 58th Street, selling beaded dresses and, after a trip to Swinging London, clothes made out of shower curtains. Morse, who died in the '70s, also ran Teeny Weeny – a small shop on Madison Avenue which sold clothes made only from synthetic materials, such as Mylar and vinyl – as well as the boutique inside Cheetah. As a result of this activity, which was spurred on by excessive amphetamine consumption and such retailing tricks as using go-go dancers as part of her window displays, she was profiled extensively in *Life* magazine. "Tiger was so ahead of her time," said actress Geraldine Smith. "No one could touch her. She made those silver short, tiny dresses. She was always on speed."

Department-store buyer Annie Flanders was inspired by Morse to open Abracadabra on East 60th Street. "She was the most incredible of all the designers and one of the first major influences on fashion in America," she says in *High On Rebellion*. "She did the first American flag shirts and had her store covered in tinfoil...She designed clothes for Jackie Kennedy and all the leading society women and then just completely went berserk. She left all her alligator handbags and fantastic thousand-dollar gowns when she got into speed and pills."

But Morse could not match Johnson for national clout. Paraphernalia franchised out to branches in cities all over the US, boosted by the flair of jewellery designer David Croland and the see-through crochet designs of Lou Reed's girlfriend Barbara Hodes. Johnson's highly commercial sensibilities and clean lines also helped to put the company on the map, particularly after Julie Christie modelled a $35 black-and-white Johnson number for *Mademoiselle* in 1966, the same year in which the actress had made a big impact in John Schlesinger's *Darling*.

In the wake of this splash, Johnson's clothes were championed by the likes of Twiggy, model Penelope Tree (who wore a Johnson creation to novelist Truman Capote's notorious black and white ball of 1966), Geraldine Chaplin, Brigitte Bardot and Raquel Welch. Janis Joplin wore a silver mini-dress made by Johnson for her first performances with Big Brother And The Holding Company, which appeared in the mid-'90s exhibition The Warhol Look, along with the velvet suit designed for John Cale.

Johnson's musical associations were everywhere: psychedelic wool knits and bikini tops were supplied by a company called Truth and Soul, which was run by Sylvain Sylvain and Billy Murcia, later to be the guitarist and drummer in The New York Dolls. Using brightly-coloured dyes and yarn from Colombia, the pair established the Truth & Soul store at 691 Broadway, where they sold skinny-rib men's and women's knitwear. "Truth & Soul, baby," ran their ad campaign. "It's honest. It's wild. It's colour. It's cool. It's love in a far-out line of threads. It's the revolution in fashion." By licensing patterns to knitting mill operator Nausbaum, the pair would later finance a dope-smoking European trip on which they encountered Kensington Market and such King's Road shops as Paradise Garage.

Meanwhile, Johnson had become disillusioned with the franchising of Paraphernalia and launched the funky Betsey Bunky Nini outlet with two

having appeared in an advertising campaign for London Fog raincoats in 1964, and one of Lou Reed's first songs – the novelty track 'Do The Ostrich' – was inspired by a column written by fashion high priestess Eugenia Sheppard, which predicted that ostrich feathers would be big that season.

As The Velvet Underground's reputation grew, so the audience that the band drew became increasingly dressed up, "glittering and reflecting in vinyl, suede and feathers, in skirts and boots and bright-coloured mesh tights and patent-leather shoes and silver and gold hip-riding mini-skirts, and the Paco Rabanne thin plastic look with the linked plastic discs in the dresses and lots of bell-bottoms and poor-boy sweaters", according to Warhol. In clubs such as Cheetah on Broadway and 53rd Street, young guys started to wear polka dot shirts with tight, flared trousers, boots and caps.

To cater to this crowd, boutiques sprang up in hitherto no-go areas, such as St Mark's Place, and the army surplus store Limbo was raided for its peacoats, sailor tops and bell-bottoms. Warhol himself stocked up on all manner of leather gear from Leather Man in Greenwich Village, while the legendary Tiger Morse – who had designed for high society before making

left Madonna in Johnson's lacy finery

colleagues. In 1971, she was designing for rock clothing company Alley Cat, and that year received a Coty Fashion Critics award for her knitwear. However, for much of the ensuing decade she felt out in the cold ("my customer had disappeared"), until punk swept through New York. Energised by this new rebelliousness, she hooked up with model Chantal Bacon, who had also lived in London, and opened the first Betsey Johnson store in New York in 1978. Others soon followed, including an outlet on LA's fashionable Melrose Avenue. By 1999, the chain consisted of 26 boutiques, including four in New York and one in London, and her label was being sold in such major department stores as Neiman Marcus and hundreds of speciality outlets. Her store in Soho turns over around $2.5 million a year, while the entire company was achieving annual sales of close to $40 million in the late '90s.

A unique sales point of the business has been the involvement of her daughter Lulu, now 25, who epitomised the company's youthful side while the orange-pigtailed Betsey symbolised the continuing restlessness of the '60s generation. Her cut-off shorts and exuberant cartwheels became a fashion-world fixture, as did her relationship with Lulu, who started modelling for her mother at the age of eight, although she opted out in 1998 to investigate opportunities as an actress or an MTV VJ. Obviously hurt at the split, Johnson has nevertheless stressed that she still consults her daughter over designing for the youth market.

In March 1999, Johnson was presented with an award by the Council of Fashion Designers of America for "her timeless talent", by which time she had branched into perfumery and beauty products and launched the

Ultra brand. There aren't many high-profile females who haven't worn Betsey, from Gillian Anderson and Minnie Driver to Helena Bonham Carter and Cameron Diaz, and she still has a loyal following in the pop and rock community. Those who have worn her clothes over recent years include Lenny Kravitz, Steve Tyler, Rod Stewart, Brandy, Lil' Kim, kd lang and Courtney Love.

Johnson has a carefully constructed business plan intended to increase annual turnover to $150 million by 2002, but she remains wistful for her days at Paraphernalia. "For five years I had nobody say 'Do this' or 'Do that,'" she told *The New York Times*. "It was so fabulous. I'd go to work every day and think, 'What do I want to wear?' If it sold, I still had a job. There was nothing negative. Now, you have to think of the negative and the positive constantly."

The involvement of Warhol's ultra-cynical and sleazy Exploding Plastic Inevitable exhibition in the so-called three-day Carnaby Street Fun Festival in Detroit at the end of 1966 underlines the impact that Swinging London was having on American pop culture. There, The Velvet Underground lined up alongside The Yardbirds and Sam The Sham And The Pharaohs at a ludicrous event which included a mod wedding, organised by the local radio station, at which the bride wore a white mini-dress and high white satin boots and the groom wore a "Carnaby uniform", which included a plaid jacket, a cowboy belt and a kipper tie.

Detroit was not alone. Youth fashion had swept through the Midwest, stimulating an entire generation to head to America's entertainment

below left & middle More of Betsey Johnson's pre-punk '70s work

below right Singer Sarah McLachlan in Johnson clothes

centres in search of fame. One such was Rodney Bingenheimer, who ran away from home in 1966. Naturally, he headed for Hollywood. "I was still at grade school – really young," he says in the inimitable low tones which have endeared him to die-hard listeners of *Rodney On The ROQ*, the show which has been running on LA alternative station K-ROQ for two decades. "I was picked up for breaking curfew a few times, and my parents came to get me, but eventually I stayed because I kind of wanted to be in a band. So I just became this kid in Hollywood, hanging around with people like The Chocolate Watchband and Sonny And Cher. They took care of me. In fact, Sonny And Cher almost raised me."

The West-Coast duo had added a distinctly American element to Carnaby; the somewhat portly Sonny Bono, then in his late '20s, squeezed himself into candy-striped hipsters, to which he added a broad-banded matelot shirt, teetering Chelsea boots and accoutrements such as sleeveless sheepskin jackets. This ensemble, along with his long dark bangs, provided an approximation of the most admired rock star in LA circles, Brian Jones, whose look was emulated to the *n*th degree by other performers, particularly The Byrds. Meanwhile Cherilyn Sarkasian played up her exotic look by acquiring a native American heritage (she is, in fact, of Armenian extraction), adopting a sub-bohemian/folk-singer look, complete with heavy, Egyptian-style make-up and a heavy fringe.

By the time that Bingenheimer had arrived in LA, there were already several stores catering to the burgeoning pop scene, situated mainly on Sunset Boulevard – particularly the Strip, between Fairfax and Doheny – and Hollywood Boulevard. On Sunset and Vine was Beau Gentry's, which

ellen von unwerth

BETSEY JOHNSON.

e & right Betsey Johnson: "It was ulous"

below Sonny And Cher "epitomised the Hollywood take on Swinging London"
bottom Nancy Sinatra: "It was a kick to be in something innovative"

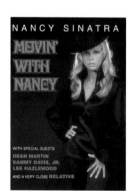

sold dandy fashions such as elephant-cord suits to the likes of Carl Wilson of The Beach Boys, while The Byrds bought capes, suede boots and granny specs there. Nearby was Cy Devore, the tailor who had produced sharkskin suits and spearpoint-collared shirts for the Rat Pack, and in the same vicinity was DeVoss, which Bingenheimer describes as "swinging mod, for your older types". Also on Sunset was North Beach Leather, where Jim Morrison bought his trousers, while Head East on the same boulevard incorporated native American designs into its clothes.

The Beverly Hills set frequented Jax on Rodeo Drive for its glamorous stagewear. The shop sold go-go boots and mini-skirts to stars such as Nancy Sinatra, who had picked up on English style via trips to London. "They were perfect for me, and I felt at home in them immediately," Sinatra says of the Carnaby Street fashions that she first encountered in 1964. "I knew that there was nothing like this new look here at home, and there were only a few people wearing the Mary Quant designs. It was a kick to be in on something completely innovative." She was also struck by the shop interiors and ways in which fashions were presented: "They were boutiques with lots of colourful patterns and prints, stripes and polka dots. It was totally obvious that this would catch on just looking at the store windows."

When Sinatra came to make her landmark TV special, *Moving With Nancy*, in 1967, Jax was the natural choice for clothes. Sally Hanson, the wife of the owner, Jack, provided designs to suit Sinatra's requirements. "We didn't have stylists then," she says. "At least, I didn't! I just shopped and chose what I thought would photograph well. Jax was the closest to what I liked best."

Meanwhile, the first fashion shop on Melrose Avenue in West Hollywood was Fred Segal, an ivy-covered establishment which continues to import the latest styles to this day, and the proximity of Lennie's Boot Parlour on Gower to the TV production company Screen Gems ensured the custom of The Monkees. Peter Tork had his puff-sleeved shirts made by the popular clothes maker Jeannie The Tailor, who was based next door to the Troubadour venue on Santa Monica Boulevard and became acquainted with many of the bands who played there. One of these, the English folk-rock exponents Fairport Convention, invited her on an ill-fated trip to the UK in 1968. Jeannie was one of the occupants of the van which crashed on the way back to London from a gig. Both she and Fairport drummer Martin Lamble were killed outright.

The young LA meeting point was the Strip's diner Ben Franks, which had become such a magnet that it was namechecked in the advert placed in *The Hollywood Reporter* by producers Bob Rafelson and Bert Schneider for auditions for *The Monkees* TV series: "Wanted: Ben Franks types…" Over lunch in his daily hang, the so-called "rock 'n' roll" Dennys on Sunset, Bingenheimer talks about how he was among the hundreds of wannabes who responded. "There were a lot of us kids who were too young to get in anywhere," he says. "We'd just be walking up and down the Strip, forming bands or promoting gigs, or just meeting up. Ben Franks was a perfect place to see everybody and find out what was happening."

Although he came close during screen tests, Bingenheimer was successful only in becoming a stand-in for the diminutive English Monkee, Davy Jones. Then, in 1966, the actor Sal Mineo dubbed Bingenheimer "the Mayor of Sunset Strip", a key role, given the fact that the historic teen "riots" had taken place on the Strip in that year, when a heavy-handed LAPD tried to put a halt to the all-night revelry. The clash between teenagers and cops was soon commemorated in the exploitation flick *Riot On Sunset Strip*, which was granted a suitably fuzz-toned soundtrack courtesy of The Standells. The event also acted as inspiration for Buffalo Springfield's unsettling single 'For What It's Worth'.

"When I got here, it was like taking part in the Renaissance," rhapsodises Joey Stec, who arrived in LA in 1967 as a 19-year-old member of Chicago group The Poor, whose ranks also included future Eagle Randy Meisner. Stec later formed sunshine pop outfit The Millennium, and was also a member of power-rock band The Blues Magoos. "From Fairfax to Doheny there were people walking up and down the Strip, flashing peace signs, passing out LSD, playing guitars. It was wild. Drugs didn't yet have a horrible criminal stigma, and we were basically all into peace and love. There was nowhere in the world like it. Hendrix would be playing at the Whiskey, The Byrds would be at Gazarri's three doors down, The Doors were at Pandora's Box – it just never stopped. At three in the morning, there were crowds everywhere."

The Sunset Strip look peaked with the riots. Thereafter, psychedelia filtered across the Atlantic, peddled in head shops such as Headquarters and Hole In The Wall. Meanwhile, Hell Bent For Leather on La Cienega catered to more abstruse tastes. (It was here that Brian Jones acquired the Nazi insignia that he wore for a 1966 photo shoot, in which he dressed as a stormtrooper.) Bingenheimer recalls taking George Harrison to an ethnic store called Satperush in Westwood: "I met him at a Ravi Shankar press conference in Hollywood and told him about Satperush, which was where the cover for The Strawberry Alarm Clock's *Incense And Peppermints* was shot. We went there, and he really liked their Indian stuff. Then we moved on to another store called Surreal Times, on Santa Monica Boulevard, where he bought a pair of heart-shaped sunglasses."

At around this time, San Francisco was emerging as a hippy haven, with tie-dye T-shirts and headbands reflecting the less glamorous and more bohemian edge of the city in contrast to Tinseltown. "It was more swinging '60s here, more dressed up," says Bingenheimer of LA. "When Granny Takes A Trip opened their branch here, there was suddenly crushed-velvet pants and satin jackets to wear with crocodile-skin shoes. We didn't really go up to Haight Ashbury that much."

One of the leading lights of the San Francisco scene was Janis Joplin, whose casual gypsy look – as displayed on the cover to her album *Pearl* – was in fact put together by Linda Gravenites, wife of harp player Mike Gravenites. The singer had left the city for an extended period in the early '60s after her career had failed to take off, and when she returned she was dressed from head to toe in workwear: Levi's, overalls – any clothing which played down the physical appearance which dissatisfied her so

much. Gravenites decided that, for Joplin to shine on stage, she should adopt the clothes which she and a handful of friends were already sporting: antique lace, silk and satin, feather boas with teased hair and a lot of jewellery. Such was Joplin's success that this look endured on the west coast for many years, and can be traced through to the stagewear worn by such performers as Stevie Nicks and Heart in the '70s and '80s.

Back in LA, a group of male musicians decided to appropriate the clothing of the wild west to suit the growing switch towards country music. A prime mover was the dandy Gram Parsons, whose International Submarine Band had worn western styles and covered Buck Owens tunes. Later, he became a short-lived member of The Byrds, and coerced them into embracing country on the 1968 masterpiece *Sweethearts Of The Rodeo*. He then flowered in his own right as the founder of The Flying Burrito Brothers, whom he persuaded to wear clothes from the flashy Nudie's Rodeo Tailors shop on Lankershim Boulevard in North Hollywood.

As Ben Fong-Torres explains in his biography of Parsons, *Hickory Wind*, the band's outfits were like nothing seen in post-psychedelic LA: Chris Ethridge wore a white suit festooned with red and yellow roses; Chris Hillman had a blue suit with satin lapels and double-breasted peacocks, whose feathers spread onto the sleeves; and steel player Sneaky Pete Kleinow wore a black jumpsuit decorated with a golden pterodactyl. Parsons' outfit, however, was the *pièce de résistance*, a short-waisted white suit covered in cannabis leaves and flowers, while the back was adorned with a red cross which sent off showers and glitter. On the lapels,

left Janis Joplin's casual gypsy look

85

right Tynedale and Rodney
Bingenheimer at his English Disco, 1973

Nudie's tailor, Manuel, had embroidered a pair of naked girls. "Somebody had to make a show of it," said Parsons.

"Nudie was the greatest guy," claims Joey Stec. "He found the way to sell country gear to rock 'n' roll people, and he made a lot of money doing it, but the real main man in all of that look was Brandon de Wilde." De Wilde was a former child actor who had starred in 1959 teen pregnancy epic Blue Denim and then became a Hollywood music industry player. Stec credits him with having helped create careers not only for The Byrds but also for The Burritos and Delaney And Bonnie. "We all used to meet at Brandon's house. Maybe it was the film Blue Denim, I don't know, but Brandon had this thing for jeans, which he'd wear with cowboy boots and a nice vintage shirt with a yoke, pearl snap buttons and those smile pockets with the darts at the end. Soon we were all wearing this stuff, going to swap meets and picking up these incredible shirts for 25¢ a pop. Gram was basically a rich kid who saw that and then had it made in gaberdine. His was like an Elvis Presley version, with the big buckle belt, jean jacket with sequins and cowboy boots with spurs, or those flat tips on the toes."

There was, however, a superstition about boots made out of snakeskin in some band circles. "We had this thing called 'the curse of the snakeskin boot'," laughs Stec. "Leon Russell's band all got a pair each – they broke up. Same happened to The Burritos and Delaney And Bonnie, so we stopped wearing them."

Stec's former bandmate Randy Meisner took certain aspects of western dress over to The Eagles, and this was transported around the world in the early '70s as the band's success grew. "It became universal," says Stec. "All of a sudden I'm landing in Holland and Germany and everyone's wearing cowboy boots and denim. It was the same then as the way we wear trainers now. And we never noticed if they were hard on our feet or not; when you're 20 years old and on cocaine, you don't care!"

The blandness and lack of imagination which was engendered by the LA cowboy look soon provoked a reaction among the dressed-up crowd. Rodney Bingenheimer was a radio promotion man for Mercury Records in the early '70s, and often worked with the latest acts from England, such as David Bowie, whom he escorted around town in the Mr Fish dress worn on the original cover of The Man Who Sold The World.

In 1972, to celebrate Britain's wave of glam rock, Bingenheimer opened his own club, the English Disco, where the sounds of The Sweet, Gary Glitter, Bowie and T. Rex accompanied all manner of decadent behaviour. Iggy Pop cut his chest with a razor there during one particularly drugged-out performance, while the rock-star likes of Led Zeppelin were entertained by nubile young things from Beverly Hills. The maverick Kim Fowley was even inspired by the club to form proto girl punk band The Runaways. Hot pants, feather boas, platforms, glitter make-up and satin, silk and velvet were de rigueur, while Rodney based his appearance on his then-hero, Rod Stewart. "He looked great then. I always admired that sort of glam mod thing he had going on," says Bingenheimer, who regularly travelled to the UK to buy clothes, including a pair of black dungarees with red stitching from Mr Freedom in Kensington.

The English Disco closed as glam faded, and Rodney went on to host his show and become a proselytiser for all manner of new music. As news filtered through that he was the subject of a documentary entitled The Mayor Of Sunset Strip, which features contributions from artists from Liam Gallagher and Courtney Love to David Bowie and Cher, Bingenheimer decided in late 1999 to reopen the doors of the English Disco. Glitter rock has since become all the rage again, and on Saturday nights in LA glammed-up youngsters pile in through the doors of the Fais Do Do night club ready for an evening's entertainment, courtesy of the ageless chap in the DJ booth who was once a teenage runaway himself.

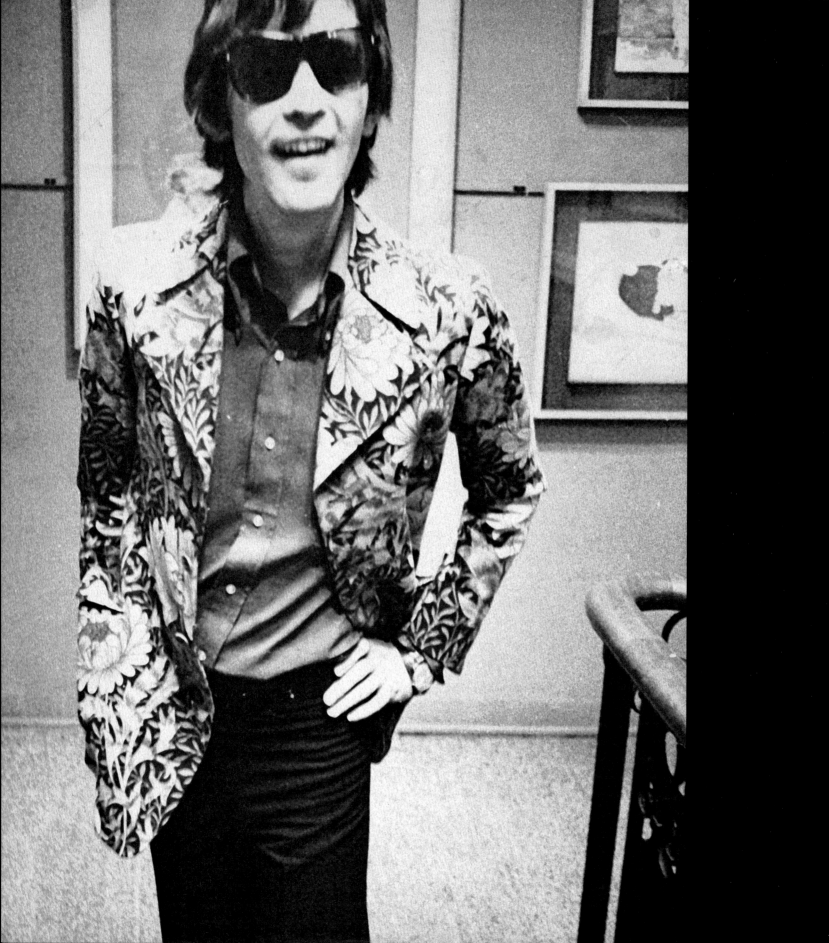

8 "Everyone Looked Like They Were A Pop Star"

As flower power disintegrated and the '60s soured, the hippy look was gradually co-opted, and within a few short years tie-dyed T-shirts, loon pants, long hair and army greatcoats were no longer the preserve of a hip few. At the same time, a more hard-nosed attitude to the commercial side of designing and selling clothes replaced the innocence embodied by the opening of, say, Granny Takes A Trip in London and Paraphernalia in New York. Style leaders of the time turned their backs on fashion now that the party was coming to a close. Nik Cohn wrote that, on one day in 1968, leading '60s scenesters Christopher Gibbs and his associate David Mlnaric "simply stopped trying".

Gibbs chuckles at the memory now. "I always thought that was very good. I liked it that Nik Cohn wrote that." He laughs. "When you're young and growing up and finding your way, these things seem important: how you present yourself when you're going to a party, etc. As life goes by, you change. There's nothing more pathetic than an old fashion victim, and I'm not one. Wasn't even a young fashion victim. I was a dandy." He explains that one of the reasons was that dressing up had lost impact: "It was incredibly easy to upset convention at one time. People wore what was expected of their professions. You could tell at a glance if someone was a solicitor or a bank clerk by the code of their dress. Now it's much less easy to work these things out."

The opening of the deeply alternative Kensington Market in late 1967, amid clouds of incense and the reek of patchouli oil in a huge five-floor building on the south side of Kensington High Street, was of course sparked by commerce rather than counter-cultural considerations; the property owners had witnessed the success of nearby Chelsea Antiques Market and decided to rent out stalls by the dozen to the underground's wannabe entrepreneurs. The warren of shops and stalls in Ken Market, as it became known, were a hive of activity for all manner of operators loosely associated with music, from blissed-out head shops and furtive dope dealers to poster companies such as Big O, run by the ever-ambitious rock promoter Harvey Goldsmith. But in their midst was a shifting cast of characters whose tiny outlets offered an eclectic range of clothing to pop stars bored of the King's Road and Carnaby Street as the '60s turned into the '70s.

"It was really buzzing between 1968 and 1971," says Lloyd Johnson, who ran a stall with his partner, Patrick Cockell. The pair were among the few who received praise from Cohn when the market opened. He noted their "ambitions to style" and the fact that they "wanted a future". This ran against the grain. For the most part, at its inception Kensington Market represented indolent hippiedom at its worst. "We used to go to Kensington Market every day, where we'd have tea, smoke hashish and buy boots all fucking day long," reminisces New York Dolls guitarist Sylvain Sylvain about a trip he made to London in 1970.

However, within the first 18 months, there were increasing signs of life, among them a stall run by future Queen singer Freddie Mercury (then Bulsara) and Spooky Tooth/Only Ones member Alan Mair, who were often assisted by Queen drummer Roger Taylor. They initially sold artwork produced by Mercury at Ealing College, and later moved into antique clothing as a means of supporting their ambitions to get their first group, Smile, off the ground.

The market also housed the talents of Ronnie Stirling and Geoff Cooper, who would later give designer Antony Price a start in the business, and whose eponymous company was also to became a force in menswear. Among the other stall-holders were the future senior Marks & Spencer womenswear executive Sheila Brown, designer Jane Whiteside and Ken Calder, who ran the outlet Ruskin. Johnny Moke was also there, along with an eclectic band comprising such diverse faces as Richard Branson's wife, Joan Templeman and Brian "Blinky" Davison, drummer in The Nice. "Basically, it was anybody who went to the Speakeasy," says Johnson, referring to London's premier late-night music business haunt. "The big look of the market became canvas zipper jackets, Budgie jackets (named after the style worn by Adam Faith in the early '70s TV series) and step-crotch jeans."

Johnson had worked at Austin Reed's Cue, where his duties included drawing clothes while sitting at an easel within the shop during opening hours. "I left there because the personnel manager kept on flicking my hair and telling me to get my hair cut," says Johnson. "I told him, 'Take your hands off me you old poof,' and was immediately sacked."

By 1967, Johnson – who had been making ties out of curtain material and supplying them via Hung On You and Granny's to acts such as The Rolling Stones and The Move – was living in west London, running with a crowd which included Krissie Findlay and her boyfriend, guitarist Ronnie Wood. He had recently disbanded Brit R&B band The Birds and was about to flit between The Creation and The Jeff Beck Group before settling in The Faces and eventually The Rolling Stones. Soon after Cockell & Johnson opened in Kensington Market, the business adopted the name Heavy Metal Kids, selling the Newman brand of stovepipe velvet jeans

imported from France and tight trousers and leather clothes made by the scene's maverick figure, Colin Bennett.

Heavy Metal Kids' exterior was mocked up like the outside of a submarine. Sprayed silver, with curved corners and fake panelling, it didn't have a door but instead a giant ovoid plug. The interior was Victorian. "A friend painted one end of the stall with the head of Medusa," says Johnson, "and on the other side there was a biker going up to a fairy castle, for some reason. It was very Jules Verne hippy-trippy. The stock fixtures were chests of drawers with clothes piling out."

A year later, the stall moved and changed concept. They were now making brightly-coloured velvet suits for the likes of Wood and Rod Stewart as artists, musicians and performers started to pour into the market. "Everyone who came in looked like a pop star," says Johnson. "We had people like Unit 4 Plus 2, Argent, The Zombies, Keith Richards, Yes, ELP. The Faces used to come round to our flat because Colin Bennett was making made-to-measure trousers and leather jackets for them." Johnson and Bennett designed the cream jacket with brown leather trim that Stewart is wearing on the inner sleeve to his 1970 solo album, *Gasoline Alley*.

One day, Mercury dropped by to invite his fellow stallholders to a showcase gig by his band, whose name was changing to Queen. "He told us and we burst out laughing," says Johnson. "I told him I thought it was a bloody awful name and would never work. Mind you, we had a guy called Rick working for us and Gary Glitter offered him a job as a bass player, but we all pissed ourselves laughing at that name as well."

Among other regulars at the market was Jimi Hendrix, who became friendly with Johnny Moke and bought a lot of stuff from his stall. Moke himself was so named because of his obsession with his car, a Mini Moke:

above Rod Stewart in a Bennett/Johnson jacket, 1970

"I had this model girlfriend, Denise. I forget her second name – it was a long time ago. She'd make the clothes and I'd buy the fabrics from Pontings." Pontings was an old-fashioned department store in Kensington, close to the site of the market, which had a large fabrics hall.

Again, the Speakeasy effect was at work: "We'd have yellow and pink velvet trousers, and somebody like Ronnie Wood would see them down there and ask to have a pair made. That's really how it started," says Moke. "Then I got to know Hendrix pretty well in 1968. I had a 26" waist in those days, and I remember I made him some trousers and he had a 30" waist, which I thought was huge at the time." Hendrix wore Moke's striped and multi-coloured corduroy trousers at the Monterey Pop Festival. In the late '90s, they fetched more than £1,000 at auction. "We were making clothes for everybody. There was no difference between what people wore on stage or on the street," says Moke, whose own appearance became increasingly outrageous. "My hair was long and dyed red, yellow, purple and green. I had a red snakeskin jacket, snakeskin boots and these trousers with no pockets to make them extra skin-tight." His stall took on a theme based on an Enid Blyton cartoon character. "Everything was Noddy In Toyland," he laughs. "We had shirts, dungarees, everything with him printed on it. Then these friends brought back Mickey Mouse watches and T-shirts from America, so we sold those. That was the kind of look I had when we got a write-up in *Petticoat* magazine."

These pop elements, among others, were to be more successfully brought together by Tommy Roberts in his first Mr Freedom store, which opened in the King's Road at around that time. Moke also created Rupert The Bear trousers out of children's curtain material, and supplied Keith Emerson – keyboard wizard with The Nice and later with ELP – with a metallic green-and-blue snakeskin suit and Marc Bolan with a sailor suit made out of a pair of vintage pyjamas dating from the '30s.

By the early '70s, many of the prime movers at the market had begun to move on. Moke joined the exodus, opening the Hollywood Clothes Shop in Fulham, west London, as a tribute to the golden age of movies. "I spent a lot of time at the National Film Theatre and the Mayfair Cinema Club watching Fred Astaire and Ginger Rogers, Dietrich, all of those. We'd go to all-nighters and drop acid."

His new store was styled like a film set. The fittings – all movable – included giant canvases portraying scenes from classic movies, cinema seats were installed and the clothes hung on mannequins of '40s film stars. The store majored in quaintly printed dresses, jackets with shoulder pads and bomber jackets. "This is all pre-Saint-Laurent; they lifted the whole collection from us," claims Moke of the Paris fashion house's '40s revival in 1970. "I found a shop selling old elastic which hadn't been used since the '50s, so we had these bomber jackets with elastic cuffs and waists. But this is how stupid I was: I decided not to do them in leather. Later, people made millions out of leather bombers." The Hollywood Clothes Shop's bombers were in Prince of Wales check featuring bold colours, such as pink or blue, with suede yokes. One became a particular favourite of George Harrison, who continued to wear it well into the '90s, while the shop's clientèle also included Fleetwood Mac and Ginger Baker.

The '40s look took off across the Western world. "Everything about the '70s was the '40s, if you think about it," says Moke. "People just don't realise it, but that's where all those wide shoulders and platforms came from." Rather than capitalise on this, however, Moke's restless spirit got the better of him, and the Hollywood Clothes Shop closed in 1972 when he opted for rural life and "became a gypsy", living in a caravan for a while before buying a farm. He would return to the business within a few years, but Moke and Johnson are both modernists who, at that time, opted to take the dandy hippy route in terms of both lifestyle and the clothes they sold. There were smarter alternatives: the two-button velvet jackets and other clothes influenced by continental Europe were popularised by shops such as Squire, Village Gate and Thackerays, along with stricter American designs which continued the lineage of Ivy League.

Having cornered the market in imported Ivy League clothes by operating the Ivy Shop in Richmond, partners John Simons and Jeff Kwintner developed and updated the look at the series of shops they ran in the late '60s and early '70s. The first of these was Squire, which opened in Soho's Brewer Street in late 1968 and maintained the American look developed at the Ivy Shop. Squire stocked beautiful knitwear, thick-soled shoes such as wingtips and plain-cap brogues, button-down shirts, Harringtons and raincoats. "Originally, Squire was totally Ivy," says Simons. "There was none of that hairy-flarey stuff around. If we did Prince of Wales check suits then it would have been to a collegiate cut."

While the first Squire shop catered to the former mods who wanted to maintain their snappy appearances in the face of the tide of faded denim and long hair washing over the Western world, there was also a growing demand among customers for more contemporary clothes influenced by continental Europe. "The flared look started to come in about 1971, as the lapels and trouser widths got wider and shirt collars became deeper and ties were fatter," says Simons. "The stereotypical thing was the three-piece suit with the concave shoulder. Prior to that, the shoulders were all convex, very American and narrow. Then suddenly the jacket had the pinched waist, there was the tight waistcoat and the trousers were much tighter around the arse. We got some of that stuff from a company called Maya in Paris."

To meet the increasing demand, Simons and Kwintner opened a second Squire shop in the King's Road, opposite the fabled Pheasantry restaurant/club, and they recruited Richard Young, who had worked for John Michael Ingram and had most recently been employed at Just Men. "I basically took over the basement to Squire and made it my world, selling the clothes I was into," says Young. "I'd discovered these Shetland cardigans - short, with belts - which we stocked and sold really well, along with velvet trousers and the two-button jackets." Simons confirms: "That was totally Richard's place, that basement, and he made it his own. It was massive - very French, with the slightly back-combed hair. It just exploded in the '70s."

The line's popularity prompted Simons and Kwintner to launch a separate brand in 1971 with a new shop in Soho's Old Compton Street called Village Gate, which was named after the fabled New York club and which betrayed their modern jazz roots. "First of all we had to phone the man who owned the club, Art Lugoff, for his permission," says Simons reverentially. "We chatted to him, and he soon realised we were jazz buffs and on the same wavelength, so he said it would be fine." Thus Village Gate was opened, and business was bright enough within a couple of years to open a second shop, again on the King's Road. "We opened that one in 1973, and I lived above," says Simons. "It was great place to have a pad. We had all the pop stars in, and there were parties everywhere, with people like Sammy Davis Jnr, Dudley Moore and Marty Feldman dropping by all the time."

By this time, the two Squire and two Village Gate shops were catering to what Simons would describe as the hairy-flarey crowd. Their success spurred on such operators as high-street chain Take Six, which had been launched on the back of the Carnaby boom by Essex-based suburban outfit Brent & Collins to mass-market the look.

Kwintner and Simons split in around 1973, with the former going for broke with the flagship Village Gate store on London's main shopping thoroughfare, Oxford Street, while Simons retained the Ivy Shop before opening a store under his own name in Covent Garden. Here he has established himself over the last two decades as the UK's premier purveyor of American and Ivy League clothes. Just ask his customers, who include Paul Weller.

The Village Gate/Squire ethos expressed the smooth, sophisticated and continental lifestyle led by a mature jazzer. It's ironic, then, that one aspect of the clothes sold by Squire contributed to the least sophisticated fashion ever: skinhead. The original elements were all imported from the US, and were very Ivy: Levi's (both denim and Sta-Prest), wingtips, button-down check shirts, crew-neck and sleeveless jumpers, cardigans, Harringtons. As it became bowdlerised in the wake of media coverage, thuggishness took over. Brogues were replaced by big boots, more likely army issue than Dr Martens, which only really came into their own during the post-punk skin revival of the late '70s. Another branch became suedehead, which dictated grown-out crops and suits in materials such as Tonik and Prince of Wales check - "Smooth, elite, expensive," as defined in the 1971 pulp novel *Suedehead* by Richard Allen. For a time, though - as singer Kevin Rowland explains here - it was a subtle and quietly subversive style created by an underclass uninterested in long-haired hippiedom.

Rowland is noted not only for his soulful songwriting and agonised vocal style but also for the attention to detail he has brought to the stylistic changes rung in both his solo career and as leader of Dexy's Midnight Runners. He continues to challenge convention; witness the cries of outrage in the UK media over his use of elements of feminine attire during the promotion of his 1999 album, *My Beauty*.

As a teenager growing up in northwest London in the late '60s, he was provided with an eyewitness view of the development of smart street fashion at that time. This is his story, the strongest thing he ever saw:

91

"Peanuts" was the only word I heard used to describe them, pre-1969. It was a mod thing to begin with, and definitely came out of that. "Top mod" used to be a compliment, as in "That's smart" – I can remember somebody saying that about a Van Heusen shirt of mine as early as 1966. The top boys in Harrow (where I lived), Willesden and Wembley were at least a couple of years older than me and looked great; they wore long gaberdine, single-breasted, fly-fronted raincoats (usually navy, sometimes beige, occasionally off-white) with fine long-sleeved crew-neck lambswool sweaters, often maroon or bottle green. V-necks would be in the same colours, but sleeveless. They also wore parallel trousers with four pleats, and many walked with their hands behind their backs.

A more casual rig-out in about 1967 was what was called a "zipper jacket", in a navy, shiny, synthetic fabric, or occasionally dark-brown suede. This had elasticated cuffs and collar and was basically an MA flying jacket, worn with a knitted shirt underneath and new-ish Levi navy blue 501s. Sometimes suits were worn, or just the jacket with a pair of Levi's. The jackets were long, three button, and only the top button would be done up, or maybe the top two. The jacket had single nine-inch to twelve-inch vents and was waisted. There would be a breast pocket and three outside pockets with sloping flaps, about an inch and a half to two inches high.

You couldn't buy such a suit off the peg, and they were made to measure in lightweight fabrics in beige, Lovatt green, fawn, or sometimes dark colours such as chocolate brown or bottle green. Ties were striped. The whole thing had a moddy shape to it. In my opinion, this look was underground in 1966 and big-ish by late '68, when Frank Sinatra-style trilby hats first became fashionable. Many had this look but with shorter hair, and this is what the media called skinhead in 1969.

That year, it started to get really American. One or two of the really smart dressers had off-centre six-inch/seven-inch vents in their jackets, patch pockets with straight flaps and raised edges on all the seams. They took the look on to a new level of Ivy League sophistication.

Some boys had their hair shaved off completely. This wasn't a numbskull look, as reported in the media, but a sophisticated fashion statement only a few would understand – middle-aged, conservative and all-American, the same as astronauts and GIs. Against the background of London in 1969, it was completely and utterly outrageous.

The same year, I noticed a couple of boys with hair slightly longer on the top of the head, parted low and neatly dressed over to one side. It tapered in to nothing at the back, instead of the more common square neck or "Boston". I understood this. It was beautiful, a variation on the all-American boy look. I realised it was a brave haircut because it would mostly be judged by the

undiscerning as very square.

I was a keen clothes watcher, and first saw that all-out American look around October 1968, when I was introduced to the Squire shop by one of the very smartest dressers in Harrow [a highly fashion-conscious area], Tim Brennan. There was hardly anybody wearing it. But what the media called skinhead was a very young thing; 16 was *the* age. In those days, working-class boys of 18 or 19 were already engaged, and by 21 they were well out of the game. It wasn't like it is now, with 30-year-olds taking part in "youth" cults. Working-class boys – and I felt this personally – had to be aware that pretty soon they would have to get serious, settle down and get married. This was a bit of fun while you were young. After that, you had to grow up. It was a conservative outlook made necessary by our backgrounds. Hippy ideas at that point had no impact whatsoever on us. The only longhairs around were middle class and considered wet, silly, not even worthy of thought or comment.

When I first saw a pair of wing-tip Royals (the plain caps were called GIs), I was shocked, because I'd been told I was being taken to this shop where the smartest dressers went. Up to that point, fashionable had meant dainty and petite, but these shoes were awkward-looking, with great big soles and heels. They were ugly, but I recognised they were also beautiful. They were outrageously expensive, too – £6 19/6, a week's wages for a lot of men. The shoes turned me on, as does the memory now. It was such a clean, beautiful look.

As I said, after that day in October 1968 I would see the occasional guy who had this subtle American look, but then it all came together in the summer of 1969. We knew we were part of something big and powerful. It was one of those things like punk or acid house, where all the factors came together at the right time: the beautiful clothes, the explosion of all those great reggae records, which we listened to exclusively. That's when I felt alive, part of something. I was aware this was my time. We danced good – often all in a line, wearing Harringtons with collars up over American-style shirts, Sta-Prest trousers with braces and brogues, loafers and Gibsons, all boys, no girls – to Return Of Django, The Liquidator, Driven Back by The Pioneers and Je t'Aime. This seemed to be the best way to pull girls, just dance good, and usually they would come near. Then, when a slow or sexy one was played, grab one.

We'd travel on a Saturday night by train over to maybe Eastcote for a dance; buying train tickets weren't an option. Girls would follow. We wouldn't encourage them, but every now and then we'd look around and they'd still be there, looking sheepish. It wasn't always like this, of course. I'm talking about the best of times.

I think the first newspaper article about all this was in *The*

top Rowland and friend, 1969: "Top mod was a compliment"

'em. I hope they felt part of something.

By the winter of 1969, some of the better-dressed boys wore trilbys and three-quarter-length sheepskins. In fact, real smart dressers had sheepskins in the winter of '68, some of them east-London West Ham supporters, or they wore navy Crombie overcoats over Prince of Wales check suits, or maybe a cardigan. Often, coats and hats would be kept on in the club. This made a great shape for dancing.

I saw my first grown-out skinhead in the late summer of 1970. I was in a club with my girlfriend, probably in the West End, and was quite shocked. He was wearing wing tips, parallel trousers and a Ben Sherman shirt, but his hair was long; it had the look of being grown out. Then my friend Pany told me about a Chelsea fan who wore skinhead clothes but had grown his hair and undid the buttons on his button-down collar, which gave it the look of a West End fashion shirt, previously most undesirable.

The writing was on the wall. Everything was changing, and it was a difficult change – for me, anyway. My hair was curly and grew outwards, and I hated it, so cropped hair had suited me perfectly. But what really pissed me off is that the cool and more subtle all-out American look I mentioned above died before it had been given a chance to grow. *This was the great lost look.* The caricatures of skinhead had prevented natural development and destroyed all subtlety, so I guess the whole progression had to fizzle and die. This is perhaps part of the reason I used this look for *Don't Stand Me Down* [Dexy's final album, released in 1985]. The other media term was suedehead, but the above would be my definition.

So hair was growing, and the shirts were the first to go. We started wearing wide collars and then penny rounds. Before long, it was the trousers and, yes, flares. Then we went for high-heeled boots, polo-necks and Budgie jackets. This was 1971, the year of transition. The "hairies" had been wearing this kind of stuff for years, but now that *we* were wearing it, it was cool. And once I'd sorted the hair out with a blow-drier and straightening tongs, it was a lot of fun getting all these dandified clothes that had previously been out of bounds for us.

It had been a difficult two years, but by 1972 it was sorted out. Transition complete. Feather cuts were in, and that summer many wore beads. One or two – myself included – wore headbands on a hot summer's day, half as a joke but with some seriousness. Again, it's hard to explain this, but it was a cool and nifty fashion statement because of the juxtaposition of the headband with people like us, who would not normally be associated with them. If a hippy wore a headband, it didn't mean anything. It was boring.

Before long, a new kind of short hair would be back. But that's a whole other story.

Daily Mirror in late summer 1969. I'd left school by this time, and one of my work colleagues told me about it. At first I was really excited and proud that we were getting recognition. I'd only heard the name skinhead once previously. A really well-dressed kid from Richmond said it to another short-haired youth. It was a jokey, slightly derogatory term, not serious. But the numbskull caricature – courtesy initially of *The Mirror* – irked. A cartoon figure dressed in a white T-shirt, braces, jeans and big boots (we only wore boots occasionally) featured in the article headed something like, "This Is A Skinhead". While it was nice to be recognised as part of something, it was misrepresented, and that ruined it basically. Just like The Sex Pistols after the Bill Grundy show – where do you go from there?

It was still fun, but I felt self-conscious. I'd feel embarrassed at work when colleagues identified me as a skinhead. Same thing with uncles and aunts. I'd feel it necessary to go into an explanation. By this time, loads of skinheads had given interviews in the national press, and I was later told by a friend from Harrow that all the interviewees had been subsequently kicked to fuck. This puzzled me and upset me, because more than anything, however snobbish I was, I was glad of the recognition, and dreamed they would interview me. It's only with hindsight I can see how the publicity fucked things up. A slightly younger version of ready-made skinheads – girls, too – appeared overnight, bless

left "In 1968 I would see the occasional guy who had this subtle American look"

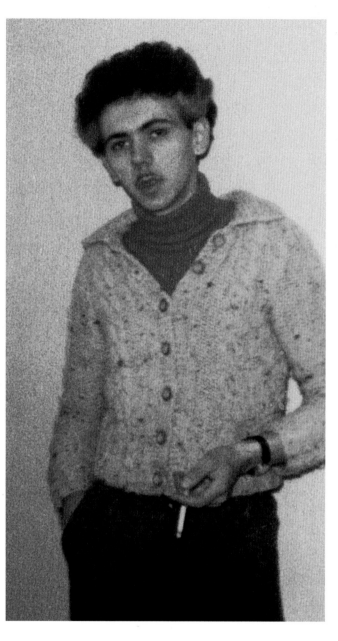

At the diametric opposite of Ivy League and skinhead in every aspect, from style to sexuality, was the nostalgia-inspired femininity and frippery of Biba, which nevertheless commanded a media presence just as powerful in the late '60s. By the time owners and husband-and-wife team Barbara Hulanicki and Stephen Fitz-Simon opened what was described by *The Sunday Times* as "the most beautiful store in the world" in Kensington High Street in September 1969, Biba had long been championed by such UK pop personalities as singer Cilla Black, *Ready, Steady, Go!* presenter Cathy McGowan and the quintessential '60s model Twiggy.

Palestine-born Hulanicki was a lowly fashion illustrator when Fitz (as he was known) suggested that they sold her designs by mail-order. Naming the company after the nickname for Hulanicki's sister, Biba was soon featured in the national press, in the summer of 1964, when Felicity Green, fashion editor in *The Daily Mirror*, picked up on a pink gingham dress called the Barbara. At 25 shillings, it was affordable yet chic, simple and mod. The dress turned Hulanicki's life around; within days, Biba was inundated with cheques and postal orders and McGowan started to show off the clothes on her show every week.

The first Biba store opened in Abingdon Road, Kensington, later that year, and was staffed by very chic and young girls with whom the clientèle identified. They wore white make-up, fringed hairstyles, mini-skirts and low-cut pumps while "their matchstick legs were encased in pale tights", as Hulanicki wrote in her memoir, *From A To Biba*.

In March 1965, Twiggy was whisked to Abingdon Road on the day after she was talent-spotted by Justin de Villeneuve at the hairdresser's at which his brother worked. "Biba's was a knockout," said the model in her autobiography. "I'd never seen anything like it before. I loved the clothes, and I loved the dark mahogany screens everywhere."

Hulanicki lays claim to having created the first fashion T-shirt by adapting a traditional women's vest, "with very high armholes and a skinny body", and Biba also dyed the woollen scarves and hats favoured by soccer fans and made them a female fashion accessory. A move to nearby Church Street in 1966 heralded the installation of the Biba deco look, with a logo created by Tony Little, who would later form interior design company Osborne & Little. This store carried the full range, from feather boas and broad-brimmed hats to underwear and gloves. Customers included actresses Mia Farrow, Barbra Streisand, Marianne Faithfull and Samantha Eggar, while Yoko Ono bought a smock dress there to cut up live on television for an art performance.

Biba rapidly expanded in the wake of this attention, its owners opening a branch in the seaside resort of Brighton and financing the 1969 move to a giant space on Kensington High Street by taking on investors, including garment manufacturer Dennis Day and high-street retailer Dorothy Perkins. The 5,000-square-foot basement in the new store was modelled after a conservatory, and the wallpaper was based on the stained glass windows in St Paul's Cathedral. Accessories were placed on painted pub tables, pillars were sprayed gold and there was a gallery in

above "This was the great lost look!"
Insets from 'Don't Stand Me Down'
right "Before long a new kind of short hair would be back"
opposite "Biba's was a knockout."
Abingdon Road, Kensington, London, 1966

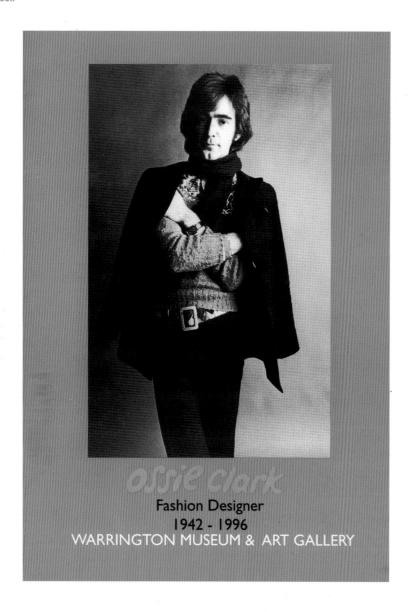

ossie clark
Fashion Designer
1942 - 1996
WARRINGTON MUSEUM & ART GALLERY

above Museum brochure
opposite "The perfect mix between sexuality and femininity"

cream and pink with velvet chaise longues. Hulanicki proceeded to stock childrenswear, and then started a cosmetics range, which was sold in 30 countries, through Dorothy Perkins outlets in the UK and Fiorucci in Italy.

However, Biba's carefully cultivated and opulent image was not to everyone's taste. In 1971, the anarchist group the Angry Brigade bombed the store as a protest against fashion's enslavement of women. Hulanicki dismissed the argument as "crazy reasoning". Undeterred, and with a rack of licensing deals around the world (including one with Bergdorf Goodman in the US), Hulanicki and Fitz embarked on the venture which would prove their undoing: taking over the huge department store Derry & Toms, which comprised 400,000 square feet of space; the 500-seater Rainbow Room, complete with stage and restaurant; and a roof garden.

Situated a few blocks down the High Street, the building could only be bought after a deal had been struck with property company British Land, which forked out £4 million to buy the outlet. Big Biba sold everything from baked beans to curtains, and is arguably the most ambitious project ever undertaken by a fashion retailer. All products carried the distinctive Biba brand in '30s gold and black, and the company even provided a banqueting service.

The Roof Garden - complete with designs courtesy of avant-garde sculptor Andrew Logan - hosted album launch parties, and many artists used the Rainbow Room for showcase gigs, from The New York Dolls, Manhattan Transfer and Cockney Rebel to George Melly, The Kinks and The Pointer Sisters.

"Big Biba started with the idea of selling the complete Them taste - jokes with everything - to a mass market but ended as a venue rather than a shop," wrote Peter York in *Harpers & Queen*. "The mass market came, but only to look. By then Biba's obvious camp had played itself out." Economic factors beyond Biba's control - the advent of the three-day working week, the collapse of the property market and growing industrial action in 1974 - posed an insurmountable threat to a new business whose financial health was already precarious. "For the first six weeks, everything ran like clockwork," was Hulanicki's memorable phrase.

After that came a long and agonising slide, exacerbated by fierce internal disputes between the founders and British Land. The result? Hulanicki was banned from entering the store and a series of emergency and cost-saving changes failed to increase turnover. Soon the ornate fittings - some of which had been specially commissioned - were auctioned off and piles of clothes were unceremoniously dumped on the floors of the half-empty halls during the closing-down sale of 1975. "When it folded, it was a massive big store with hardly anything in it," says customer and former Sex Pistols bassist Glen Matlock. "The kids' section had been done up like Sleeping Beauty's castle, with her all laid out on a bed. Later on, when we played Andrew Logan's party (one of the first Pistols gigs), he had it all stacked up around us at his warehouse. He'd obviously taken it back there." There have been several attempts to revive the Biba name over the intervening years, most recently in the mid '90s, but all have failed. Hulanicki now resides in the US.

Biba was very much a store of its time, and it's possible that the fashion contribution it made may have been overstated in the light of the hoo-ha surrounding the Derry & Toms fiasco. Certainly, this is the view of rival retailer Tommy Roberts of Mr Freedom, who once utilised the charms of the Rainbow Room to showcase his charges Kilburn And The High Roads: "Biba was not what you'd describe as an award-winning design affair. The dress that everyone goes on about was actually very simple, only two seams and that's it. Also, the menswear was absolutely atrocious, but for the time it was right. Taking ideas from Victoriana or whatever and finding old fabric isn't design. If you want somebody who really changed things, you'd have to look at Ossie Clark. He was the best we ever had."

On a barge moored in the network of canals Little Venice in spring 1966, Ossie Clark held a stunning show of his latest ethereal creations for Quorum. It was a natural step for the music-mad Clark to draw on the energy and showmanship of rock, but by doing so he was unwittingly heralding a new era for the fashion business. Out went the snooty calm and staged ceremony established by the giant European houses in favour of "a happening", according to his textile designer wife, Celia Birtwell. "That's the only way I can describe it," says the soft-spoken Birtwell at the premises of her charming fabrics and furnishings business in trendy Notting Hill. "It was a happening. We'd actually had one at the Revolution club a few months earlier, but that Little Venice show really changed everything, even down to what type of models were used. Ossie was the first to have black models wearing his clothes, and soon everyone else followed."

John Pearse concurs: "Ossie Clark's shows were amazing. They would put anything you see today to shame – Alexander McQueen, anybody – if he had half the budget they have now."

Antony Price, the future designer of Roxy Music's clothes, who started at the Royal College of Art in 1964 (the year that Clark left), mourns the fact that there is virtually no surviving evidence of the shows. "They were devastating and very new and very rock business. His shows were also very different to little ladies dragging fur coats. The models were stoned on the catwalk in these amazing outfits. He did about ten shows, some in Paris, but I went through *Vogue*'s archive and they covered him twice, which is criminal because he was the most influential of us all and really made the whole rock music thing happen. He wore eccentric, fabulous clothes himself, and was at the centre of that whole scene in Ladbroke Grove, with people like Miss Hockney floating around stoned in blue-silver Rivieras."

Music permeated Clark's life and informed his work, as Lady Henrietta Rous, Clark's friend and the editor of his diaries, wrote in 1998: "Ossie was the first designer to fuse rock music and fashion, and this wild combination seared into contemporary consciousness."

He was both a fan and an intimate of the rock aristocracy, having excitedly attended The Beatles' 1964 gig at the Hollywood Bowl in Los Angeles as a personal guest of Brian Epstein. There were musical

reputation as a creative genius in the field of female fashion, with chiffon dresses and use of *crêpe de chine*, gauze and raw silk, was complemented by distinctly rock 'n' roll clothing such as hot pants, jackets in snakeskin and leather and bomber jackets.

"Ossie Clark captured the perfect mix between sexuality and femininity," wrote Stella McCartney in the brochure for the splendid retrospective of the designer's work and life held at Warrington Museum and Art Gallery, in the town in which he was brought up and where he attended college.

"Ossie's always been known as this feminine designer because he was so fantastic at cutting and realising his ideas about how women should dress and what fitted their bodies," says Birtwell, whose contribution to the Clark canon cannot be underestimated. Her choice of fabrics and prints was as essential as his design and cutting genius. "Everyone seems to forget now that he also came up with really hard-looking, rocky clothes. We had these leather bike jackets, like the ones Brando wore in *The Wild One*, in a lot of different colours and materials. They were absolutely beautiful."

The stir caused by Clark's clothes plunged him into a *milieu* comprising the likes of Chelita Secunda, the former *Nova* fashion editor and wife of band manager Tony Secunda; Pattie Boyd, model and partner of George Harrison and Eric Clapton; and Marianne Faithfull, all of whom enthusiastically took part in his fashion shows. John Lennon and Yoko Ono sent him flowers and best wishes for the most spectacular of these, held at Chelsea Town Hall in 1969, where the music was organised by T. Rex manager and Pink Floyd agent Tony Howard.

"When I first met him, he was actually quite camp," says Birtwell of the bisexual Clark, "but as the '60s wore on he started to grow his hair and wear those big leather belts and look quite macho in his own way. He really looked as much like a rock star as the people who came to our shop, and I think that side of his life took over his persona to a certain extent."

Birtwell has never been a fan of The Rolling Stones ("I always thought it was better when black people did it, personally"), but the band became closely associated with Clark. Brian Jones intermittently lived above the shop in Radnor Walk, ordering floral shirts by the dozen, according to Lady Henrietta Rous. Jones also introduced bandmate Keith Richards to Quorum's printed satins and skin-tight jewel-coloured trousers, and Clark was such a firm friend of the ousted Stone that they spoke on the day that Jones drowned in his swimming pool, 3 July 1969.

Although Ossie Clark was backstage at the free concert that The Rolling Stones gave in Hyde Park a few days later, he did not in fact make the "male dress" worn by Jagger. This was supplied by Michael Fish, who also produced the long dress worn by David Bowie on the original cover of *The Man Who Sold The World* in the following year.

Clark's first encounter with Mick Jagger was engineered by Marianne Faithfull, and it proved a revelatory experience for the designer. As he wrote in his diaries, "My first sight of Jumping Jack Flash was his tongue, which appeared from behind the curtain of the two changing rooms,

connections everywhere in his life. Even Quorum's van driver was future Pink Floyd guitarist Dave Gilmour, who "just used to stand around", according to Birtwell. "He never really said very much. It was a bit unnerving." She goes on: "Ossie was mad about music. In the '60s, he'd buy six records a week, and we'd listen to them all the time: Cream; Crosby, Stills And Nash; The Beatles. I can remember putting together my first collection to *Sgt Pepper*; it was very important to us. But the ones which stick in my mind are the ones which kept you awake until two o'clock in the morning, like Jimi Hendrix, who I always had an aversion to because he was always being played [at] the wrong time of the day."

Such was Clark's wayward lifestyle. He had long been mixing in music and art circles – one of his RCA contemporaries was David Hockney, and an early girlfriend was Jenny Dearden ("the ultimate '60s rock chick with long blond hair and purple crushed-velvet trouser suit", according to Birtwell), who would later marry Small Faces frontman Steve Marriott. His first substantial media coverage, in 1965, centred on a silk satin coat which incorporated elements of pop art and psychedelia. In that same year, he left the RCA, having also come up with such designs as an op-art catsuit and a white PVC coat which featured flashing lights.

Clark's *entrée* into the London fashion world came via Alice Pollock's Quorum, which opened in Ansdell Street, Kensington, in 1964. "She was selling all these lacy things and children's clothes and really needed a designer with strong ideas, which is what she found in Ossie," says Birtwell. "I only had one piece as part of his first collection, a scarf with a cubist print which I poured everything I had into."

In the wake of the excitement caused by the Little Venice show, Quorum moved to Radnor Walk, just off the King's Road, where Clark's

above Jagger's "dress" was in fact designed by Michael Fish

followed by his face, which broke into the grin I was destined to know so well." They soon collaborated on Jagger's performance clothes, including his red and black leather jackets with streamers attached. Among Clark's more notorious designs were the wedding dress supplied to Bianca, which allowed her nipples to peep out during the nuptial ceremony, and the series of skin-tight glam jumpsuits that the singer wore for The Stones' notoriously drug-addled 1972 tour of the US. He also made the diabolic black cape worn by Jagger at the disastrous Altamont Festival in 1969.

In the following year, those present at the Quorum show at Chelsea included Jimi Hendrix and photographer Cecil Beaton, who listened to the soundtrack provided by the likes of The Steve Miller Band and British blues/prog outfit Juicy Lucy, and in 1972 Clark's superstar status was confirmed by David Hockney's portrait of himself and Birtwell, which now hangs in the Tate Gallery. His re-invention of the '30s bias-cut dress has been an enduring influence, notably on such contemporary designers as John Galliano.

The early '70s were the peak for Clark. Within a few short years, his personal problems, poor grip on finances and heavy drug abuse had taken their toll. In the wake of punk, Clark appeared to be a man out of time, as is depressingly chronicled in his diaries. However, the '90s witnessed a reawakening of his art, and he later worked with fans such as Bella Freud and Ghost founder Tanya Sarne and made an appearance as a model at a Comme des Garçons show in Paris, and an ankle-length '60s snakeskin coat of his design was included in the RCA centenary exhibition in February 1996. Sadly, existing in severely reduced circumstances, Clark was murdered less than six months later by his psychotic lover, Diego Cogolato.

Birtwell's favourite photograph of Clark dates from his heyday in July 1970. His hair is expensively coiffed at medium length and he's wearing aviator shades, a T-shirt and a zip-up snakeskin biker jacket. Clark looks every inch the pop star. "I love that photo," sighs Birtwell. "It really sums Ossie up."

I CREATORI DELLA MODA
PETER GOLDING

In questa pagina: un completo in jersey chiné grigio-nero, con camicia stampata a giardino. Nelle foto piccole, in alto, la camicia ad aeroplanini è indossata sotto la camicia-jeans con tasche sagomate; in basso, un completo pelle-di-pesca beige con una camicia a donnine-fumetto. Nella pagina accanto: color tabacco il blouson in grossa maglia a coste; in fustagno albicocca i pantaloni con decalcomania al bordo; bianca e nera la camicia. Tutto disegnato da Peter Golding per Jesus-Beatrix Diffusion.

left Peter Golding in *L'Uomo Vogue*, 1971

107

above Ace assistants model animal
prints and hot pants

opposite "It was a great suit - Bowie
just wore it and wore it"

London, from the aforementioned Mercury *et al* to Marianne Faithfull, Jerry Hall, Lulu, David and Angie Bowie, Gary Glitter, Britt Ekland, Bryan Ferry, David Essex and Elton John. "If you want to play the fashion card with a pack of aces up your sleeve, wear a Cartier watch with a pair of Peter Golding jeans and you'll be in the very best company," proclaimed the *Fashion Guide* in 1977.

Such acclaim powered a move to 193 King's Road, which doubled the retail space and provided them with a large basement. "This may be the hottest store in the world," raved the *European Fashion Guide*, which compared shopping at the store to a visit to the then-trendy Bond's disco. "The black walls shine under silver lights, music plays continuously and there's no telling what stars might pop in."

Within a couple of years, another Ace had opened on London's fashionable South Molton Street. "Ace in South Molton Street didn't really run because the real fraternity was in the King's Road," says Golding. "You got fashion people there, which wasn't the same thing." By the time Ace shut up shop in 1985, however, Golding had established an impressive international network which he sustains to this day, mainly on the back of such successful innovations as his stretch jeans, which were worn by the likes of Janet Jackson and Cher.

All the while maintaining his hobby as a collector of rock art and posters and his interest in the blues (Indigo Records released his debut album, *Stretching The Blues*, a couple of years back), Golding says that Ace was very much of its time, and laughs about the occasion that he approached the legendary Nudie Cohn of Hollywood and asked him to supply glitzy westernwear to his shop: "He was sitting in his store in north Hollywood and I said, 'Mr Nudie, I have a shop in London and I think we can work together. I have a lot of high-profile clients, and we could promote your clothes for you.' He looked at me and went, 'You wanna buy, you buy. You wanna sell, you sell.' And that was that!"

Meanwhile, back at City Lights in 1973, Tommy Roberts came up with probably his most enduring design: a man's suit with flared trousers, turn-ups and a box jacket, as worn by David Bowie on the sleeve of his 1973 covers album, *Pin-Ups*. "It was a great suit," says Roberts. "Bowie just wore it and wore it. We had to have it copied about 50 times for him because he loved it so much. Angie and David were really keen on the shop. They'd come in and buy one of everything." Bowie and his wife were not the only habitués of City Lights from the music business, and Tommy decided to increase his involvement by getting into band management, via a curious and circuitous route.

Through his licensing of the rights to the cartoon character Rupert The Bear, Roberts had made his first contacts in the business when he struck upon the idea of releasing a single to promote his clothing line. Sadly, the details are lost in the mists of time. "I worked with this bloke who done a song which got played on *Children's Hour*," he says vaguely, "but then they pulled it because Paul McCartney had been talking about doing one, and they knew he would wipe the floor with it." Whether Roberts is referring to

DISTRIBUTED BY Minos Matsas & Son C⁰ L͞t͞d

the track 'Rupert', which charted in 1971 for Jackie Lee (who also scored with the single 'White Horses' as Jacky in 1968), we'll never know, but what is certain is that the experience whetted his appetite.

"Funnily enough, it sounds a bit cocky now, but I had this idea for a sort of boy band," he guffaws. "The thing was supposed to be three or four young blokes performing in singlets, throwing a medicine ball about the stage or skipping with ropes inside a boxing ring." While pitching this notion (an extraordinary concept now, let alone in 1973) Roberts was brought into contact with the crazed Arthur Brown, whose career path had been on the slide in the years after his eccentric 1968 Number One hit 'Fire'. "Somehow he was on the scene, and I got him a record deal," says Tommy, a deal which eventually resulted in the best-forgotten album *Dance*, released on Gull Records in 1974, "but he was such a fucking arsehole to work with that he couldn't do it. From that, Ian [Dury] got in contact, came round to my house and asked me to manage Kilburn And The High Roads."

That collection of aging art-school misfits were the furthest that a group could be from a boy band. Mixing music-hall rudery with '50s rock 'n' roll and pre-punk vigour, The Kilburns commanded an unlikely and deeply uncommercial visual presence: frontman Dury had been stricken with polio at an early age, the drummer played from a wheelchair, and the bassist was a dwarf. Dury's bittersweet urban vignettes were sung in a gruff cockney bark, while he and his band wore stage clothes which mixed jumble-sale clobber with East End flash. "We looked unique, dressed unique," said Dury in one of his last interviews. "We were all art-school babies who knew what we were doing. We were sharper than Bryan Ferry because we come from London, not Newcastle, with due respect: sharp, man, on the case. We weren't designer because we bought second hand. But back then, second hand was wide open. We were trendy on about four occasions in about four years. We got trendy later on when we got Tommy Roberts as our manager."

Although at the forefront of the grass-roots pub-rock movement, The Kilburns had fallen out with record company Warner Music, which refused to release an album recorded for subsidiary label Raft. In the spring of 1974, their manager Charlie Gillett opted to concentrate on his career as a broadcaster and journalist. Enter Tommy Roberts: "I thought, 'Fuck me, this is a little bit different. But I knew Ian was talented and clever. I sussed that Warners would get rid of them for anything – they couldn't bear to even have them on the premises – so I took them on."

Under Roberts' guidance, The Kilburns recorded an album for Dawn Records. *Handsome* is a patchy affair, but it nevertheless underscores Dury's crafty lyrical genius and the band's musical edge, which contributed towards the sound of punk. Fans included The Sex Pistols – who were corralled into witnessing The Kilburns live by Malcolm McLaren – and members of the new ska band Madness. Stand-out tracks include 'Pam's Moods', a paean to pre-menstrual tension, and the single 'Rough Kids'.

"'Rough Kids' was a great record, but before it's time," says Tommy, shaking his head. "We just couldn't get it played on the radio." Visually,

Kilburn And The High Roads benefited from the alliance with Roberts. He commissioned Let It Rock to make grey, double-breasted zoot suits for the band while he supplied velvet-collared suits in Licorice Allsort prints and even an embroidered boxer's gown for Dury. "Tommy got Malcolm to make us a bit of kit," recalled Dury. "He never paid anybody, so that was funny. He made me a boxer's dressing gown with 'Billy Bentley' written on the back, after the character in one of our songs. One of our early managers, Charlie Gillett, he got the idea about our image being important, that we were based on the idea of the band as looking different, and informing the music that way."

For a showcase performance at the Chelsea Cinema in King's Road (which housed the original run of *The Rocky Horror Show*), Roberts organised a spectacular backdrop of the Thames vista towards Tower Bridge, which drove home their urban image. The band then set off on an incessant round of live gigs.

But Kilburn And The High Roads were too rich and rough-hewn a mixture for the anodyne mid '70s, and after about a year Roberts gave up the ghost. "Somebody said we should do something more bluesy, and I was, like, 'Fucking blues? I can't bear the blues!' It just petered out after that. I realised it wasn't the world I wanted to be in." After a brief shot as Ian Dury And The Kilburns, the singer went solo and, under new management, recorded the landmark 1977 album *New Boots And Panties*. This became an astounding critical and commercial success, and paved the way for a distinguished pop and acting career cut cruelly short by cancer in March 2000. "I was delighted that *New Boots And Panties* was such a success for Ian," says Tommy. "It just wasn't suitable for me, and it was better that he went off and did his own thing."

During Tommy's time handling The Kilburns, City Lights became a draw for groups of Oriental visitors. "We always had all these Japanese designers checking us out from when we were in the King's Road," says Roberts. "They'd come in to have a look and really liked all the pop stuff. When it changed to City Lights they were a bit put off first of all, and then became really interested."

Japanese influences on Western fashion had started to emerge after the landmark 1970 show at the Great Gear Trading Company by Kansai Yamamoto, whose work was available via the Boston 151 store. By 1972, Issey Miyake was selling through leading outlet Escalade, and the designs picked up where Roberts had left off, as noted by *Nova*: "Funny, colourful pop on sale...Miyake dislikes reviving old fashions. He thinks from top to bottom, designing the accessories, clothes and undies." However, their interest in designing a total look, as well as taking the muted colours and less structured approach of City Lights, wasn't enough to sustain the business. "Covent Garden was still a vegetable market. The shop was impossible to find," admits Tommy, whose employment policy didn't help matters. "I had this big Frenchwoman in a big hat working there, and she really frightened people. It was too esoteric, too obscure. I think I was right, but the shop should have been in a more accessible position."

In the spring of 1975, Roberts closed down City Lights. Within 18 months, the Roxy Club had opened in Covent Garden and established itself as the centre for live punk performances, and within a couple of years clubs such as Hell had sprung up in the area, acting as the seedbeds for the coming new romantic explosion. By the beginning of the '80s, shops, bars, restaurants, advertising agencies and all manner of media companies proliferated.

The closure of City Lights meant that not only was Roberts out of Covent Garden but that he was also out of the rag trade for good. He chose instead to develop his interest in retro and antique furniture, exporting container-loads to the US. When Rod Stewart went through a phase of collecting Tiffany lamps and art nouveau in the mid '70s, under the influence of his partner, Britt Ekland, the singer consulted Tommy; and when Led Zeppelin guitarist Jimmy Page built a collection of vintage What The Butler Saw machines, Tommy advised him on the sources.

Roberts continues to work in this capacity for the likes of Eurythmics founder Dave Stewart, and his company, Tom-Tom, thrives. There has been one brief flicker of a return to fashion: in the mid '90s, surfwear designer Shawn Stussy struck a deal with Roberts to revive a number of the images originally sold at Mr Freedom. The run sold out, despite complications in the production process.

Tommy still conforms to the description of him by Nik Cohn nearly 30 years ago: "He's an amiable fat man from Catford, a bit of a slag, and conspicuously so, but shrewd, funny and hard to dislike." He's happy at Tom-Tom, consulting on private collections and helping architects outdo their partners with fashionable retro office furniture. But there is a hint that some day he might make a full return to the clothing business. This time around it is to be hoped that Roberts' richness of ideas will for once be in sync with the market. "I've still got the name," he says nonchalantly. "You never know, I might do it all again."

10 "Kids Have A Hankering To Be Part Of A Movement"

In 1969, Malcolm Edwards – at 23 an apparently perennial art student – and his partner, 28-year-old junior-school teacher Vivienne Westwood, took to the occasional shopping excursion along the King's Road, home of their favourite haunt, Mr Freedom.

Tommy Roberts' pop take on the '50s had sent their interest in clothes into overdrive. On one visit, Westwood bought a lurid green dress and a frilled skirt; on another, a pair of leopardskin-print velvet trousers. Such purchases inspired her to start making her own clothes in brassy fabrics from vintage patterns. These were to be the first tentative steps on her path to becoming the cleverest and most innovative designer of the late 20th century.

McLaren (as Edwards named himself two years later) once bought a pair of Mr Freedom shoes: blue suede, D-ring lace-up brothel creepers, quilted on top. An insignificant act in itself, but the effect on him was seismic. "Mr Freedom was a very important shop at that time, and those shoes were probably the most important things I have ever bought," says McLaren now, eyes a-glitter at the memory. "I had been at various art schools by then, and to buy a pair of blue suede shoes made a statement about what everyone else was wearing and thinking. It was a symbolic act to wear them; that's what I felt as I walked down the King's Road."

With his elongated vowels shifting as ever between aristocratic camp and East End barrow boy, outbursts of manic tittering and now-greying but still curly red mop of hair, McLaren talks loudly above the hubbub of the student bar at the London School of Economics, on the campaign trail for his mischievous but ill-fated bid for the title of Mayor of London in the early spring of 2000. Dressed in a dark suit – simultaneously dandyish and sober – and a French-style raincoat, McLaren stands out a mile from the throng, who regard him at a distance in their dress-down combats and trainers. Tellingly, he struggles to obtain anything approaching sophisticated refreshment. Having struck out requesting a Bloody Mary and then a Campari and soda from the barmaid, he settles for bottled water. "Blimey," he giggles. "Guess that'll teach me to order such '60s drinks."

The reawakening of an interest in rock 'n' roll style occurred at a key period for both him and Westwood. By 1969, he had spent six years switching courses and renewing grant aid at various London art colleges, while she held a desultory series of jobs and concentrated on bringing up their children, Ben (from her first marriage) and Joe (her son with McLaren). At the time, McLaren was emerging from prolonged immersion in contemporary art and subversive ideologies, which combined in his affiliation to the Situationists, France's political pranksters whose theories revolved around the dehumanising effects of consumerism and contemporary culture.

However, at this time the student protest and public insurrection of May 1968 was fast dissipating, and the pair looked about them for new sources of inspiration. They had avoided involvement in popular stylistic and musical developments for many years. Hippies were sneered at as "hippos", and McLaren declared that he had finished with pop music when The Rolling Stones moved beyond the grubby R&B clubs and pubs of Soho and west London. "I remember seeing them in some club near Leicester Square," he recalls. "They were known for wearing those matelot shirts, which made that London-Paris connection with the Left Bank. But this time they had on white shirts which were actually very dirty. This seemed thrilling to me; it made them sexy, outlaws."

In terms of dress during the '60s, McLaren had stuck to a somewhat dandified appearance, which centred on sporting a brightly-coloured tartan scarf in reference to his Scottish roots. According to fellow student and friend Fred Vermorel, McLaren's contemporaries remember little remarkable about his appearance beyond an oversized yellow boiler suit run up for him by Westwood.

Mr Freedom also provided McLaren with a direct line to the youthful spirit of early rock in the form of a character known as Harry The Ted, a shop assistant employed by Tommy Roberts largely to add atmosphere to his establishment when it moved to Kensington. Harry dressed in tight, dirty jeans, a string vest and big boots or a drape suit and creepers, and his hair was done in a greasy quiff. He also hailed from Harrow, the bastion of ted-dom and the London suburb where McLaren had once attended college and where he had also met Westwood. "Harry was a total ted, beyond total, fucking mental," chuckles Roberts. "He was good image. I was into the image. Harry didn't care who our customers were. There'd be Jill St John or some film star looking through clothes and he'd go, 'Wot you fuckin' doin' with that rack, cock?!' He'd say to David Hockney, 'So you want a pair of trousis, do yer, cocker?' He gave the shop a wonderful feel."

Johnny Moke, who at that time was running the Hollywood Clothes Shop in nearby Fulham, believes that Harry may have provided a spark for McLaren. "We all used to go out together, and Harry was a bit younger than us and out to impress. He'd be there all dressed up and talking about being a Teddy boy. He was a bit of a handful, but we all really liked him and Malcolm was always paying attention."

opposite Jordan, Seditionaries, 1977

Whatever, there is no doubt that, by the end of the '60s, McLaren and Westwood had settled on pure rock 'n' roll as a means of expressing their disgust with the post-hippy fall-out. McLaren spent the late '60s collecting hundreds of original rock 'n' roll singles and '50s artefacts and ephemera from flea-market stalls and the dusty shelves of old shops in far-flung suburbs. While Westwood sold home-made jewellery on the Portobello Road, he also tinkered with an historical film about London's main shopping thoroughfare, Oxford Street, some of which was shot inside Mr Freedom. Unfinished, this work included a tribute to the most vital British rock 'n' roller, Billy Fury, whose manager, Larry Parnes, was another of McLaren's heroes.

"Malcolm was such a character, portraying himself as this street-smart ted whilst discussing dadaist art," recalls Gene Krell in his book on Westwood. "I have never encountered a more diverse mentality, or such a Walter Mitty-ish existence. Vivienne was another matter: so stunning, so incredibly stunning, with a lovely curvaceous body, beautifully shaped legs and an intense manner of speaking."

In late 1971, McLaren was on the hunt for premises to sell his collection, and dressed in a blue lamé '50s-style suit made for him by Westwood (so the story goes), he took a walk along the length of the King's Road until he encountered Paradise Garage at number 430. The shop was on its uppers and ripe for renewal. Owner Trevor Miles had disappeared on an extended break, and his stand-in, Bradley Mendelsohn, struck a deal with McLaren, Westwood and their art-school friend Patrick Casey to take over the back part of the store in order to sell refurbished radios, records and clothes.

In his own words, this was "a chance rendezvous", although this doesn't account for the fact that McLaren knew the site well from its Mr Freedom days, and was also likely to have known that Paradise Garage was not exactly thriving. Certainly, when Miles returned in a rage at being usurped and threw out their stock onto the pavement, the pair turned immediately to Tommy Roberts. The shop's former owner provided a lawyer, who ousted Miles from the scene.

"Fashion seemed to be the place where music and art came together," McLaren offers as an explanation for his transformation from deadbeat student into revolutionary retailer. "Creating my own clothes was like jumping into the musical end of painting. The shop became a natural extension of my studio. I was very anti-careeristic and, in my head, I was promoting failure."

below Let It Rock customer Chris Spedding

Casey and McLaren set about overhauling the shop while Westwood worked away at producing a line of copies of the original clothing which McLaren was amassing. A sign was erected displaying the legend "Let It Rock" (after the Chuck Berry song) surrounded by musical notes, picked out in pink on black corrugated iron. With the ted revival under way, the shop had a ready-made clientèle, whose brutish charms appealed to their renegade sensibilities. There was a jukebox left over from the Mr Freedom days, and this survived every subsequent incarnation of the shop until its refit in late 1976 to become Seditionaries, and much of the

initial stock of Eddie Cochran and Billy Fury records remained until well into the punk years.

"The back sales area was painted black," wrote Jon Savage in his exhaustive story of The Sex Pistols and punk, *England's Dreaming*. "The clothes were hung on an antique stand; they were a mixture of vintage items and reconstructions – the trousers made by Vivienne, the jackets by an East-End tailor named Sid Green. Other items included blue and silver pegged pants, several scarlet shirts and a beautiful '50s flecked jacket, in black with white strands woven in like TV static. Dotted around were Day-Glo socks, vintage records and handbills for films such as *Rock Around The Clock*, *Vive Le Rock* and *The Damned*.

"The front half of the shop was the hangout area. This was dominated by Odeon wallpaper and a peculiar *trompe-l'oeil* window under which stood an original '50s cabinet, picked out in pink taffeta and containing plastic earrings, Brylcreem and pendants. On top of this sat a picture of [crazed early-'60s novelty rocker Screaming Lord] Sutch, his hair flying wildly as though from electric shock. On the wall, Billy Fury leered from within a garish glass frame."

Some of the clothes and artefacts were supplied by Leicester-based dealer Steph Raynor, later John Krevine's partner in founding Acme Attractions and Boy. His friend David Parkinson, a photographer, had heard about McLaren's plans for Let It Rock, and took Raynor along before the refit had taken place. Parkinson worked for softcore porn magazine *Club International*, and took many photographs of the shop from its earliest days. He died after jumping out of a moving train compartment in the mid '70s.

"Malcolm was in the middle of working out what to do with it at that stage," says Raynor. "Then, when we went back a few weeks later, it was up and running. Entering the shop felt like entering the set of a '50s B-movie. There were old teds, dwarfs and generally disfigured people just hanging around. There was a little sign outside, Bakelite radios on the street and lurex trousers. I know the favourite thing he had at that time – which he wouldn't sell – was a black *Rock Around The Clock* shirt with alarm clocks all over it. I told him I could get some bits and pieces, and we had a working relationship. I'd drive a VW to London and he'd be upside-down in the back rooting through things."

The shop soon attracted media attention, with features appearing in the national UK press and *Rolling Stone*, and its profile was bolstered by a commission to provide clothes for Ringo Starr and David Essex in the 1972 movie *That'll Be The Day*. One of the first customers, buying stacks of '50s records, was future advertising supremo and art patron Charles Saatchi.

As Patrick Casey faded from the scene, McLaren became the huckster boutique frontman while Westwood stayed at their flat in the south London neighbourhood of Clapham and toiled assiduously, all the while thoroughly researching period detail and use of cloth. "Let It Rock had magic, but that's a lot to do with the fact that Vivienne had magic," says Roberts. "She always worked really hard at getting her clothes exactly right."

Vive Le Rock gave its title to one of the first screen-printed T-shirts produced by the pair when they took a stall at the London Rock 'n' Roll Show at Wembley Stadium in the summer of 1972. Printed in white on black, the slogan appeared on the front of the shirt in a banner over a picture of a rampant Little Richard, while on the back an image of Jerry Lee Lewis appeared under the words "The Killer Rocks On".

The bill, which attracted an audience of 50,000 fans, featured an odd mixture. There were veterans, including Fury, Lewis, Little Richard, Bo Diddley and Brit rocker Heinz (whose backing band that day became pub rockers Dr Feelgood), but also relative newcomers such as Gary Glitter and The MC5. The latter performers received an aggressive reception: "Hardcore teds are lobbing the cans everywhere," wrote Douglas Gordon in a stream-of-consciousness review in the underground magazine *Frendz*. "Gary Glitter: present-day rocker rep in the Top Ten...fatal after MC5...brown ale's flying everywhere..."

The Vive Le Rock T-shirt failed to sell, and the unsold stock was converted into knickers. Westwood was to wear a pair in a 1975 *Club International* photo shoot on the shop, in which she appeared along with assistants Alan Jones, Chrissie Hynde and Jordan. The Vive Le Rock design was retained and later adapted with additions of recipes from *The Anarchist's Cookbook* and a quote from '30s Spanish anarchist Durutti: "We are not in the least afraid of the ruins." The original was a particular favourite of Sid Vicious, who wears one in the promo video for 'Pretty Vacant'.

But the failure to cash in at Wembley was less significant to the pair than the reactionary attitude of the teds to the newer performers. Not that McLaren or Westwood had any sympathies with The MC5 or Glitter, but such conservatism soon began to wear thin when customers criticised any attempts to expand the range beyond the traditional ted outfit. This provoked the duo into action, and in 1973 Let It Rock was recast as a rocker hangout, operating under a new name: Too Fast To Live Too Young To Die. While it continued to sell drape suits at £70 each and brothel creepers in a variety of styles, extraordinary original designs started to creep onto the shelves.

From black leather biker jackets with chains to custom-made zoot suits, McLaren had started to extend his interest in cult clothes, but always with a twist. The tailor Sid Green had a story that McLaren once brought a suit to him and asked him to copy it. Green pointed out that there was a kink in the shoulder but McLaren insisted that the imperfection should remain, and thereafter the shop's suits retained that kink.

Westwood supplied a number of sleeveless T-shirt designs, all in black. One range had zippers placed over the nipples, while another extended the cap sleeves revived by Antony Price at Plaza by placing small cut-up rubber tyres over the shoulders. Some had simple statements such as "SCUM" printed on them, while on others "Venus" was spelled out in studs on the front and the garment festooned with horsehair on the shoulders and zippers, again over the nipples. There are now very few of these in existence; '80s pop star and avid clothes fan Pete Burns of Dead Or Alive has one, and another hangs in pride of place in a Notting Hill

collectors' emporium, where the owner refuses to sell it for any offer.

Even these designs were outdone by the very limited range of T-shirts featuring chicken bones which spelled out "Perv" and "Rock". In her Westwood biography, *An Unfashionable Life*, writer Jane Mulvagh says that only a dozen of these were made, one of which was bought by Alice Cooper.

Although the shop had undergone its name change for a considerable time by 1973, it still retained the Let It Rock title in the window, a fact which served to bemuse one particular youth who stumbled inside in search of a pair of creepers on a Saturday morning that year. "That was one of the first times I'd been down the King's Road," says Glen Matlock, sitting in the calm of his basement flat in Maida Vale, west London, where he has been working on a new solo album. "I was looking for a pair of brothel creepers because for a time they became a bit of a thing for skins to wear. I don't know why. Then I found a pair in the window of this shop which seemed to have two names."

Brought up in the Irish-Caribbean enclave of Kensal Green, Matlock was then a 16-year-old grammar schoolboy, an avid football and music fan who admired The Faces, in particular the nonchalant dress sense of bassist Ronnie "Plonk" Lane. "I wasn't really a skin. I wasn't really anything. Just used to pick up on different looks," shrugs Matlock. "I used to go to shops like Mr Freedom in Kensington. That's where I bought this Elvis Presley short-sleeved shirt which had 'Return To Sender' written on it. I'd never seen anything like that before. My mum washed it and it shrunk to nothing."

In the event, Matlock didn't buy a pair of creepers at 430 King's Road that day, but he was so struck by the interior décor ("it looked like my granny's sitting room") that he asked for a job as a Saturday boy and was hired on the spot at the rate of £3 10s a day. "It was basically still Teddy boy stuff then, although they had just started doing the chicken-bone shirts," says Matlock. "On Saturday mornings, you'd turn up pretty late and there'd be this queue of people wanting to buy the creepers which had been delivered from Cox's the night before. They'd all be gone by the middle of the afternoon."

On his first day at work, Matlock dressed in his best clothes: a three-piece corduroy suit from Take Six. It was immediately obvious that this would not fit in with his new environment. "I started wearing their gear: straight trousers, a mohair sweater and these shirts which were copied from a Vince's Man Shop catalogue. They had Capri cut-away collars and elasticated waists." The design came from one of the many vintage porn, pop and clothing magazines and pamphlets strewn around the shop, which Matlock was encouraged to read and absorb as part of his education in the seamy side of popular culture.

He recalls being taken to venues and sites from rock's heyday, including an authentic '50s coffee bar called the Macabre, in deepest Soho. "I don't know how Malcolm knew about it, but it was the real thing. The tables were coffin lids and the jukebox only had songs to do with death," enthuses Matlock, who embraced such cult experiences but nevertheless needed counselling in the wiles of retailing. During his first months as assistant, he would receive weekly calls from Tommy Roberts asking how much money the shop had taken. "But then Malcolm put me right and I kept my mouth shut after that."

There had been growing tension between McLaren and Roberts, which was exacerbated over a dispute, possibly regarding payment of a set of zoot suits that Let It Rock had supplied for Kilburn And The High Roads. When Roberts' warehouse was burgled and his most popular line – the box-cut suits worn by David Bowie on the back cover of *Pin Ups* – was stolen, the finger pointed at future Sex Pistols guitarist Steve Jones and his friend Wally Nightingale, both habitués of number 430 and both with reputations for thievery. "Steve and Wally had stacks and stacks of these jackets," laughs Matlock. "They offered me one for a fiver. I didn't buy one. A, I wasn't that keen on them, and B, it was the last thing I could wear in Malcolm's shop."

For his part, Roberts is still smarting. "That bloke in The Sex Pistols came and apologised ten years later," he snorts. "I said, 'Don't fucking apologise now, it's too late, old son.' I won't go into it; there was a reason for all that. It was to do with jealousy. They wanted us out of the way. As it happens, by that time I'd had enough of it all, anyway. I'd made my statement."

As the teds withdrew their custom, so the clientèle became more diverse. "When they began doing the zoot suits and the peg trousers, all these blokes from west London started coming in," says Matlock. "They were the kind of guys that had jobs but lived at home with their mums and drove big American cars. They were definitely a bit more interesting than the teds, who just used to stand there looking hard."

The shop's visitors were indeed an eclectic bunch. The artist Andrew Logan and the ballet dancer Rudolf Nureyev were as likely to drop in as heir John Paul Getty and broadcaster/journalist Janet Street Porter, while musicians who bought articles of the ready-made stagewear included the magnificently shambolic and drugged-up New York Dolls, whom McLaren attempted to manage for a spell in 1974-5.

Dolls guitarist Sylvain Sylvain had long been acquainted with the store. A fashion retailer in New York in a previous incarnation, he had bought "groovy threads" at Paradise Garage while on shopping trips to the UK in the early '70s, when he became friendly with Trevor Miles. McLaren and Westwood met the band in August 1973 at a New York fashion fair, where buyers were by and large stoutly unimpressed with their wares. The Dolls, on the other hand, loved them. "They had some great things: Jerry Lee Lewis underpants...and all these English-style '50s shirts, like Billy Fury and Adam Faith would have worn," says Dolls associate Peter Jordan in Nina Antonia's biography of the doomed group, *Too Much Too Soon*. A party was held in The Dolls' honour in the couple's room at the Chelsea Hotel. "They scattered all these softcore lingerie magazines around. We went up there and stole everything we could get our hands on."

"The first time I saw them, [The New York Dolls were] supporting The Faces at Wembley," says Matlock. "Not long after, I went with Malcolm to see them at the Rainbow Room. He went to Paris and eventually followed them to New York." McLaren's attempt to revive The Dolls' career is well documented, including as it does the decision to relaunch their image as card-wielding communists in red leather and cire. The band split amid drug- and alcohol-fuelled acrimony, and their wannabe manager returned to London feeling dejected.

At this stage, Matlock had been participating in scrappy band rehearsals on stolen equipment with Jones as vocalist, Nightingale on guitar and their friend Paul Cook on drums. They shared a common bond, not only in the shop but also in liking The Faces, but Matlock was also keen on another group of pre-punk pioneers, The Sensational Alex Harvey Band. A visit by members of that group to the shop revealed to Matlock not only McLaren's paranoia about business affairs at that time but also his lack of knowledge of the drawing power of contemporary rock acts. "I was chuffed when they came in, and was serving away when Malcolm started getting really edgy. He told me to get rid of them, so I had to tell them we were closing early. Once they were gone, he insisted that they were tax inspectors on the snoop. I kept on telling him they were a big rock band, but he wouldn't have it."

A few weeks, later Matlock coerced McLaren and his friend Bernie Rhodes – the future manager of The Clash, who had sold second-hand clothes in Chelsea Antiques Market – into accompanying him to a SAHB performance at the Hammersmith Odeon. "It was absolutely packed with these kids, and that's when I think the penny dropped with Malcolm. That coincided with us getting the band together and being more on the case, and Malcolm realising that The Dolls had had it."

When Matlock began his attendance at St Martin's College of Art, he pestered McLaren to sign his entry form. "He kept on ducking it. Eventually, Vivienne did it in the end. She told me it was best that Malcolm didn't sign it because he'd been slung out of every art school going."

In the early summer of 1974, Westwood and McLaren decided to invent the shop anew as a fetish and bondage outlet, inspired in part by their recent visit to New York. This trip had opened their eyes to the outsider status of sexual deviancy, which, now as then, has a far greater capacity to shock than youth cults. In that April, in an interview in the *NME*, McLaren talked of clothes "getting more transsexual" and mused over the notion of persuading radical psychiatrist RD Laing to design suits for the store.

The shop underwent a prolonged refit, and the fact that it was closed for months did not best please the impecunious Matlock. "I kept on ringing Malcolm all the time, and he told me that it was taking longer than they thought." This isn't surprising; when it reopened in September 1974, the transformation was total. Outside, the name "Sex" was emblazoned in four-feet-high pink rubber capitals and sprayed with slogans from Valerie Solanas' SCUM (Society for Cutting Up Men) manifesto, as well as situationist slogans and quotes from the drug-addicted outsider pornographer Alexander Trocchi.

As Jane Mulvagh details, the clothes – Westwood-adapted lingerie, hoods, leather- and bondagewear – were hung from gym exercise bars placed along the walls, along with whips, chains, nipple clamps *et al.* From the ceiling were fixed swathes of ominously ballooning pink surgical rubber, while mannequin torsos – sometimes naked, sometimes clad in bulging cire briefs – were crammed higgledy-piggledy in the window.

This pays homage not only to Vince's Man Shop in the '50s but also to the subterranean gay shops which operated in the equally oppressive climate of the mid '70s, one of which, London Leatherman, acted as an inspiration. Situated on Queenstown Road, directly on the route from Westwood and McLaren's Clapham home to the shop, its façade consisted of wooden panels surrounding a one-foot-square window displaying a mannequin's trunk garbed in tight leather shorts. The image was at once forbidding and thought-provoking.

Sex was more openly provocative. Above the entrance was sprayed a Rousseau maxim which had been considered as a name for the shop: "Craft must have clothes but Truth loves to go naked." "The Sex shop people, untypically, have political views, of a kind which they describe as anarchic," wrote Peter York in *Harpers & Queen*. "[They] hate Retro, and seem perfectly sincere about it, but they are working in a 1958 Council Flat Greaseball vein. In the graffiti décor sprayed in their shop appears the telling question: "Does passion end in fashion?"

McLaren predicted in an interview in short-lived rock paper *Street Life* (a UK attempt at *Rolling Stone*) that the shop would start a cult: "I think now that kids have a hankering to be part of a movement, like Teddy boys in the '50s and mods in the '60s," he told writer Rick Skymanski. "They want to be the same, to associate with a movement that's hard and tough and in the open, like the clothes we're selling here." In the picture accompanying the article, the youthful McLaren is wearing a grubby white shirt emblazoned with the stencilled situationist motto "Be Reasonable – Demand The Impossible."

The story was put around that Mick Jagger had tried to enter the shop but had had the door slammed in his face in a gesture of defiance to the old order. "Now, this is all total fantasy," Jagger told the *NME*. "I don't even know where the Sex shop is...Hold on, I vaguely recall where Let It Rock used to be. But there's a lot of clothes shops in the King's Road, dear, and I've seen 'em all come and go. No one ever slams the door on me in the King's Road. They all know I'm the only one who's got any money to spend on their crappy clothes. Though even I would draw the line on spending money on torn T-shirts!"

Matlock helped to erect the Sex sign and sprayed some of the slogans, including '68 aphorisms such as "Under the paving stones, the beach" and *"Prenez-vous ça que vous désire pour la réalité"*, but was "a bit miffed" to find that he had been replaced as an assistant by Chrissie Hynde. The future Pretenders leader had struck up a friendship with the Sex crowd and tired of her job as a journalist with the *NME*. However, within a few weeks, Hynde was also out; suspecting her of infidelity, her boyfriend at the time – the elegantly wasted rock scribe Nick Kent –

top McLaren (hooded) with Pistols acolyte Helen Wallington-Lloyd

left Acme's new brutalism

119

right Lining up for *Club International*, 1975. (L-r) Steve Jones, unknown, Alan Jones, Chrissie Hynde, Jordan, Vivienne Westwood

attacked her at the store one evening, whipping her with his belt. McLaren dispensed with her services and Matlock was rehired

Kent was one of the loose retinue of musicians who rehearsed with Matlock, Jones and Cook before they recruited John Lydon (who became Johnny Rotten) in late August 1975. "When Malcolm came back from New York, he brought back all these flyers from CBGB's: pictures of Richard Hell with his hair all cut up and wearing ripped clothes, that picture of the early Heartbreakers with tomato-ketchup wounds," says Matlock. "We actually had a correspondence with Hell about him joining us. One day, Bernie [Rhodes] said he saw this guy who had that look in the area, and then he walked into the shop."

The Sex Pistols were born a few days later, as Rotten writhed and struck mock-horror poses accompanied by Alice Cooper's 'I'm 18' during an post-pub "audition" at the shop. After a faltering start, the group's incendiary energy soon attracted media and record-company attention, and as the group's commitments grew so Matlock's attendance record worsened. Meanwhile, his place at the shop had been taken by Jordan, the assistant whose individual take on dressing up ensured that Sex began to receive the attention it so richly deserved.

Travelling to central London from the south coast every morning wearing spike heels, stockings and rubberwear and with an electric-shock blonde beehive and outrageous make-up, Jordan became as much of an attraction at the shop as the clothes, particularly since her obvious intelligence and ready wit provided a counterpoint to Westwood's schoolmarmish persona. "Me and Jordan sort of crossed over," says Matlock. "I left after I got in really late one day and Vivienne started shouting at me, 'It's not just a job working here, you know. It's a privilege. You've got to understand that.'"

Westwood's hectoring tone aside, there is little to dispute in the statement. The Sex range of original clothes more than matched the bondage- and leatherwear bought in from such specialist suppliers as Estelle and She-An-Me. The shop still carried elements of the past lines, such as the shoes, mohair jumpers, zoot trousers and Levi 501s, but the sum total was nothing less than revolutionary, and tailor-made for an emerging group aiming to upturn a turgid music scene. Sex jeans in red, blue and black polished cotton had rubber zips and PVC patch pockets with a zip inside, and the mohair jumpers began to feature holes and lopsided patterns while shirts were ripped and scorched. McLaren's inventiveness was evinced by designs such as the slingback boots which were attached at the heel by a white strap.

These and other clothes from the shop were all worn by Pistols members throughout the group's existence, although Rotten maintained the DIY look which had scored him the gig. (He was noted not only for his green hair and ripped clothing but also for his ripped Pink Floyd T-shirt, which had been adapted with the words "I Hate" above the band logo.) But the insurgent spirit of Sex was best expressed by the shop's T-shirts, which collectively represent a startling and subversive worldview.

When he started at St Martin's, Matlock was urged to use the college's facilities to produce screens for the increasing number of shocking designs needed to accompany Westwood's latest creation: a sleeveless T-shirt made from two squares of cloth with the seams on display. Bernie Rhodes was on hand not only to help with the screen-printing of the T-shirts but also to supply a stream of ideas.

Gone were the days of merely reproducing the images of such '50s stars as Eddie Cochran. Over a period of around two years, as Too Young To Live evolved into Sex, the team at number 430 produced a tight and concise range of less than 20 shirt designs, in which icons were overturned, sexual imagery was overtly displayed, scores were settled and outlaws were celebrated. Priced between £2 and £5 each, the T-shirts were printed on stark colours – black, white, pink and red – with zips and cigarette burns added and holes strategically ripped. Despite the relative freedom of expression in the new millennium, there are several which still cannot be worn today without provoking public comment. Among the most notable in the collection were the following:

Sex Pistols
The lettering spells out the band's name in capitals over swirls of pink and green and a duplicated photograph of a naked pubescent boy exhaling smoke from a cigarette held in his left hand. The image was taken from a UK paedophile contact publication, one of the many sex mags scattered around the premises of Sex. The design was worn by Jones and Rotten during their first round of rehearsals and at certain gigs in late 1975/early 1976.

Lonesome Cowboys
The image of two cowpokes, naked from the waist down apart from their boots, with huge penises dangling enticingly close to each other, was accompanied by the following misspelled dialogue: "Ello Joe, been anywhere lately?" "Nah, its all played aht Bill getin to straight." Within days of the first designs being produced, in August 1975, Sex shop assistant Alan Jones was arrested while wearing one in Piccadilly Circus. Charged with "exposing to public view an indecent exhibition", McLaren and Westwood claimed that they were later fined, but Jones says that he had to pay the £30 penalty when they failed to turn up in court. The shirt remains a strong seller and, when relaunched by McLaren's export-only label, Dead In England, in the late '90s, was worn by such celebrities as singer Robbie Williams and Oasis leader Noel Gallagher's fashion-plate wife Meg Mathews.

You're Gonna Wake Up One Morning And Know Which Side Of The Bed You've Been Lying On...
This manifesto of 430 King's Road, attributed to Rhodes and Westwood, was issued in November 1974 as a statement of intent, delineating the shop's hates and loves in a typewritten list which washes in colour from red to blue. As we have already seen, the first group majors on such '60s figures as Granny Takes A Trip founder Nigel Waymouth and his wife Nicki, as well as Chelita Secunda and Pauline Fordham. Thus the "Hates" comprise the sacred cows of the old school from various areas: music – Bryan Ferry, Leo Sayer, David Essex, Yes, Elton John, Rod Stewart ("Oh for money and an audience"), *Top Of The Pops*; the media – *Honey*, *Vogue*, *Harpers & Queen*; and fashion – Stirling Cooper, Jean Junction, Browns, Take Six, C&A and Biba – "Old clothes, old ideas and all this resting-in-the-country business".

Among the "Loves", however, there are no fashion references but a strong contingent of black musicians, as well as rock 'n' rollers, cults and a few contemporary acts. This category includes Eddie Cochran, Jamaican rude boys, Archie Shepp, Bob Marley, Jimi Hendrix, Sam Cooke, King Tubby's Sound System, dreadlocks and zoot suits, Jim Morrison, Guy Stevens records, Iggy Pop, Spunky James Brown, Marianne Faithfull, Gene Vincent and Kutie Jones and his own Sex Pistols.

I Groaned...
With zips over the nipples, this was also produced in 1974 on lurid pink with a quote taken from Trocchi's book of lesbian fantasies, *School For Wives*, written in the same script as the heading to "You're Gonna Wake Up..."

Basketball Player
One of the T-shirts for which Matlock produced the screens on college equipment, this displays a naked black basketball player – sometimes overprinted with porn excerpts – with an elongated penis. Vicious wore

above Steve Jones sports a "Fuck Yr Mother" T-shirt, 1977

one with a sparkling Acme Attractions dinner jacket at early Sex Pistols concerts, while Rotten wore one when The Pistols performed at Andrew Logan's Alternative Miss World Party at a warehouse in south London in February 1976.

TITS

"One of Westwood and McLaren's most brilliant early designs," says Jon Savage about this use of a photograph of female breasts printed at the wearer's chest height to unnerving effect. A particular favourite of drummer Paul Cook.

CAMBRIDGE RAPIST

Among the shop's most disturbing products. Sex manager Michael Collins had been interviewed by police when it was suspected that this mid-'70s serial rapist – who preyed on young students – had purchased his leather hood from the shop (although there are strong indications that the troublemaking McLaren himself had informed the police). The T-shirt shows the hood in black and green, with the musically annotated quote "It's Been A Hard Day's Night..." Underneath is a fake news-wire excerpt reporting the death of Brian Epstein in 1967, which says that The Beatles' manager's demise was due to "taking part in sado-masochistic practices/S&M made him feel at home."

On other T-shirts, the commodification of childhood was explored: Mickey and Minnie Mouse were shown enthusiastically enjoying sexual congress, while a startled Snow White engages in an orgy with the Seven Dwarfs, in a savage overhaul of Mr Freedom's celebration of the pop innocence of these images. Chelsea police once impounded all of the Snow White T-shirts from the shop after complaints from passersby. "I received a frantic call from Vivienne and went down to the police station to sort it out," recalls lawyer Nick Pedgrift. "I managed to sweet-talk the desk sergeant into dropping any charges and handing back the shirts. When Vivienne arrived, she was furious and complained that I had spoiled her chances of appearing on the six o'clock news."

As time wore on, sexual deviancy and political insurrection became the orders of the day. The "Destroy" T-shirt – which, like many others, also appeared in a muslin version as part of the new range when Sex became Seditionaries in late 1976 – featured the slogan over a swastika, an inverted crucifix and the Queen's head on a postage stamp, while underneath appeared lyrics from the Sex Pistols song 'Pretty Vacant'. And the assault on icons continued apace; one shirt, "Piss Marilyn", depicted a urine-soaked Monroe.

After 1977, the T-shirts became vehicles for more calculated outrage and, as such, lost potency. At the end of that year, McLaren ordered a number from a gay sex shop in San Francisco which included the Mickey and Minnie design and another depicting a cartoon scene of gay men fist-fucking under the exhortation, "Fuck Yr Mother...And Run Away Punk!" Meanwhile, a gay punk orgy entitled "Prick Up Your Ears" contains a quote from Joe Orton's Diaries - "...I'm from the gutter so don't you forget it because I won't" - and the death of Sid Vicious' girlfriend Nancy Spungen was commemorated with a rush-released shirt displaying the bassist clutching roses under the words, "She's Dead. I'm Alive. I'm Yours." The apotheosis was reached when Westwood used both sides of a shirt for a rant against Derek Jarman's "punk" film *Jubilee*, which matched the film by being tediously overextended.

Sex and its clothing rubbed up against the grain of the anodyne mid '70s. More than half a decade after the heyday of hippy, patchwork denim, flared trousers, afghan coats, cheesecloth shirts, cowboy boots, velvet jackets and clogs had become a uniform as much as platforms, Oxford bags and satin bomber jackets. To wear small-collared shirts and narrow trousers was remarkable enough in those days, but the clothes at number 430 King's Road went much further, by making an overt statement. "I had a strange idea of fashion at that time," said Clash guitarist Mick Jones in a BBC documentary made in 1989. "I would totter round with long hair and wear women's high-heeled shoes, but also I'd wear a Sex shop T-shirt. I must have looked ridiculous, but I didn't care."

There was, however, one other store which bucked the trends and gave Sex a run for its money, but Acme Attractions - run by Steph Raynor and John Krevine - represented a much more inclusive and multi-cultural prospect. The outlet has a very important place in the evolution of fashion and music in the '70s, but its story has never been told in detail, cast as it is in the shadow of McLaren and Westwood's activities.

"If you think about it, it's all Sha Na Na's fault," says Raynor over sausage and mash in a cafe in Spitalfields Market, City of London, where his company, the Lifestyle Co, trades in retro furniture, which he describes as "what we have always sold - 20th-century-style pieces". Sha Na Na were the rock 'n' roll revival act who took to the stage at the Woodstock Festival with the exhortation, "OK, you fuckin' hippies, we're here to tell you that rock 'n' roll is here to stay." In tight, gold lurex, wraparound shades and greasy quiffs, Sha Na Na's New York flick-knife gang attitude was always more interesting than the pedestrian cover versions they peddled. At a London gig in 1973, according to Tommy Roberts, Vivienne Westwood jumped up on stage and jived with them.

"Just seeing them in the film of Woodstock triggered something," says Raynor, who in 1971 was dealing in Americana - vintage cars and jukeboxes as well as original British rock 'n' roll clothing. "There was a sea of these Crosby, Stills And Nash bands around, and they came on and just told them to fuck off."

A former mod who had never quite shaken his roots (on the hippy trail he "pissed off all these people" by having clothes made to measure in Istanbul street markets), by the dawn of the '70s Raynor was a canny clothes collector with an unerring eye for detail: "You've got to understand [that] nostalgia didn't exist in those days. We were into locating pieces which were almost art: Tommy Steele jackets, demob suits, straight-leg Levi's in black with red stitching, winkle-pickers. I'd go into

shops in Leicester, Nottingham, wherever, assess the situation and get some brilliant stuff.

"We also used to get really dressed up ourselves. It's very interesting doing that, like being a pop star without all the bollocks, the manager shit. People pay attention when they see you and think, 'This guy is something.' There was a small pack of us in Nottingham, Leicester, Manchester and London. We were just doing Purple Hearts and living it large."

On one afternoon in early 1972, after selling some clothes to Let It Rock, Raynor was strolling down the King's Road dressed in a white flecked suit, white winkle-pickers and a hand-painted tie. "This guy on the other side of the road came running across and asked me about myself because he said I looked so interesting," says Raynor. "We started talking, and he invited me to lunch and bought me fish and chips." His host that lunchtime was John Krevine, who had a shop in south London's Brixton which sold one-arm bandits, pinball machines,

above Steph Raynor: "We were doing Purple Hearts and living it large"

123

jukeboxes and vintage radios. However, the shop's location was wrong, and Krevine – who now lives in Israel, and was unavailable for interview – was not faring too well. Within months, the pair had joined forces on a new venture, a stall selling retro lamps and furniture inside Antiquarius, the antiques market on the King's Road.

"It was right in the middle," says Raynor. "What with John's warped sense of humour, I'm sure he found it very funny that all the others were selling fusty old antiques and we were selling these pop culture things. We had a rail of clothing – Burberry macs, flecked jackets, shoes – and we sold out on the first day. The objects were completely static; they just didn't move. Now it's flipped around and furniture is fashion, and you can't get arrested with clothes."

Trading under the new name Acme Attractions, the stall shifted to the back of the market early in 1973, and, with a jukebox and a scooter installed and demob suits pinned to the wall, Raynor and Krevine concentrated on the clothes. A customer of Krevine's Brixton outlet, Don Letts, managed the stall. "I'd gone into that shop because it was so weird; there was nothing like it around Brixton," says Letts, then an 16-year-old grammar schoolboy who had gained some sales experience while working at the King's Road branch of Jean Machine, the most successful of the denim boom shops. "Back in the day Jean Machine was pretty cool," he says, "there were all sorts of freaky and hip people working there: gays, dykes, drug addicts. We used to have a right laugh, going to all the parties and hanging out with the people from Paradise Garage and Alkasura."

With the jukebox filled with dub reggae singles and customers such as Ian Dury buying demob suits, the stall was a success, but the other Antiquarius occupants were extremely unhappy that the rarefied

atmosphere had been disturbed. "The jukebox pissed everyone off," says Raynor. "It was a combination of that and wanting to expand which took us downstairs. It was a Pat Boone period, when they start releasing that pappy shit and everyone's waiting for something to happen. There was still a lot of long hair and Afghan coats floating around, getting mad with us because we were driving around in wraparound shades and short hair in big American cars. They'd be spitting on us, they were so upset!"

So Acme moved again in 1973, into the basement of the market, where its subterranean nature – combined with booming U-Roy and the scent of weed – was complemented by all manner of new and second-hand clothes: short-sleeved sports shirts, zoot suits, mohair three-button suits, pork-pie hats, tab-collared pinhole shirts, brothel creepers and the Marlowe crêpe-soled shoes favoured by Steve McQueen.

The shop was managed by Letts and his girlfriend, Jeanette Lee (who would later join Lydon's group Public Image Ltd), and one of Acme's main attractions was the scooter, the same model as that owned by Sal Mineo's character in *Rebel Without A Cause*. The most popular lines were the range of winkle-pickers and peg trousers cut by Tony Daniels, one of the same tailors used by Vivienne Westwood. The pegs retailed at £12 and were available in a range of materials, from pearl grey to electric blue and shocking pink.

Many who entered via the dangerously steep staircase would become stars in their own right – Chrissie Hynde, The Clash, John Lydon, Sid Vicious, Patti Smith and Bob Marley, to name but a few – and its popularity was increased not only because there was always the possibility of scoring some cannabis on the side but also because it presented a less austere approach than 430 King's Road. David Parkinson took a picture of a group

below Cheesecloth and patchwork denim ruled the ad pages of *NME*, 1975

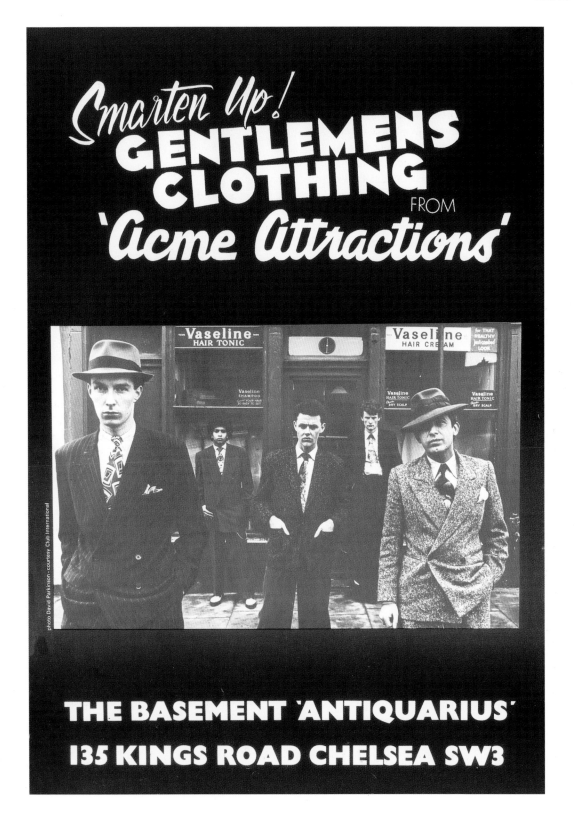

including Letts, Krevine, Raynor and customer Martin Brading (now a photographer in his own right), lined up wearing zoot suits. This was used as part of a promotional poster displayed around London.

"Acme was much more than a shop; it was a club, a lifestyle, an attitude, a forum for talent," says Letts about the premises where he first encountered Clash guitarist Mick Jones, with whom he would form Big Audio Dynamite in the '80s. "I basically made it like my living room, with a sofa and lots of '50s knick-knacks and my sounds blasting out. We had such a laugh there. The guys would all be in to see Jeanette, and we knew everyone at all the other shops, so we'd be doing little deals for records and clothes. I think I can honestly say that Acme, in the basement, was the happiest time of my life. Selling clothes, although a major part of it, became smaller than the main business, which was the social interaction between the different cultures. We'd have the soul boys coming into town in their big cars and then mixing with the south London wide boys or girls who wanted to buy plastic raincoats and stilettos, and they'd all be in there listening to 'Dreadlock Dread' by Big Youth and 'MPLA' by Tapper Zukie."

Two such were brothers Jay and Phil Strongman, who had plugged into retro fashions via their interest in funk music played at such out-of-town venues as the 666 Club in the Horley Hotel, Berkshire. "At the 666, they would drop a Bowie or Roxy track in as well as the funk," says Jay, now a journalist/DJ and the brains behind lounge/samples act Sophisticated Savage. "Everyone was moving out of platforms and Oxford bags into '40s suits and slim-line trousers, which coincided with Bowie's *Young American* look and Roxy's GI uniforms. I started going to Acme because I saw a couple of guys wearing shiny-grey peg trousers, plastic sandals and a cap-sleeved T-shirt with a handkerchief done up at the neck. They told me to go to Antiquarius, but I could never find the shop."

One day, Strongman was in black music record shop Contempo in the West End and noticed the Acme promotional poster. He made straight for the address on it. "It was a completely life-changing experience, walking down those stairs. I'd never really heard heavy dub reggae before, and on the walls were great '50s prints of gay guys in Harlem wearing suits and make-up and all these peg trousers pinned up to the walls. Don had his dreads and was wearing tigerskin shoes and peg trousers. Jeanette was wearing this micro mini-skirt, really '60s. Every fashion that had happened up until that point was there – Beatle suits, everything. You got to meet people from all over the country – they'd come from Glasgow, even. The customers were basically everyone who was bored with what was going on."

His brother Phil, a writer whose novel *Cocaine* is currently being developed for film production, recalls the attention to detail at Acme: "The clothes that they stocked, from the '40s, '50s and '60s, were all incredible. A lot of them still boxed up and shrink-wrapped, in pristine condition. Acme was like a secret society – the scene was so small its regular customers probably numbered no more than 250-300 people. The police never bothered to go there, so all sorts would be happening. Don Letts would be smoking dope – the kind of thing you just couldn't get away with,

top right Jay Strongman in "Anarchy" shirt, 1977

middle Strongman in 1975: "Acme was life-changing"

bottom Pre-mod revival Strongman, 1975

below Bowie's besuited *Young Americans* look

opposite Acme Attractions: soul boy meets punk

These and other connections made at Acme would propel Letts into different media. When he was asked to DJ at the opening of first and foremost punk club the Roxy at the end of 1976, he took along the only records he had, which were obscure reggae tracks. Thus dub became the soundtrack of choice at punk gigs, while artists such as Marley, Dennis Brown, Junior Murvin and Burning Spear were granted a receptive mainstream audience largely due to Letts' evangelism.

He also became the scene's official film historian. Having been given a Super-8 camera by stylist Caroline Baker (who later became fashion director at *The Sunday Times*), he shot many exciting performances from the DJ booth at the Roxy and assembled them in the landmark documentary *Punk Rock Movie*. This provided Letts with his *entrée* into the film world, in which he is still very much involved. Having shot more than 400 promo videos, his recent work includes the movie *Dancehall Queen*, which focused on the fashions and lifestyle surrounding the Jamaican dancehall scene in the '90s, as well as The Clash retrospective *Westway To The World*.

There were distinctive Acme looks: vintage short-sleeved shirts, plastic sandals or winkle-pickers and brightly-coloured mohair jumpers were picked up by the soul boys and became one clubbing style, as did the demob suits worn during the brief Glenn Miller revival of 1975. Acme was a mecca for those who would later get into jazz funk and electro and form the new romantic coterie: club-runners Chris Sullivan, Ollie O'Donnell, Steve Strange and writer Robert Elms. The premises even hosted one soul boy's wedding.

However, Acme's diverse range ensured that it survived fads: "We had an office with a [one]-way mirror, and we'd sit in there watching and pissing ourselves because we were so excited at how busy it was," says Raynor. "There were queues around the block within two weeks of opening. I'd get home some nights and I'd have thousands of pounds to count out all over the carpet."

Letts argues that Acme "reflected the way London was going. It was about multi-culturalism, whereas Vivienne and Malcolm were always more Eurocentric." Raynor concurs: "Don was pioneering that. It was so cutting-edge you couldn't breathe. People would come into the shop and just stand there, listening to the music. Vivienne and Malcolm wouldn't know what dub was. We were pumping out music at a sound and volume which they couldn't compete with. You'd go down there and it would still be Billy Fury. We took our cue from the dance-floor."

There had always been rivalry between the Westwood/McLaren camp and Krevine/Raynor's. In fact, there is a story that the latter pair surreptitiously followed McLaren to his tailor so that they could use him to make peg trousers. Raynor, however, denies this: "The truth is, there was this very charismatic guy called Vic who went back a long way with Malcolm. He was really magnetic and switched on to all the aspects of East End tailoring. Vic knew every tuck, fold, crease, button-placing, but he and Malcolm fell out and he came to us and turned us on to the same tailor."

in those days – and second-hand goods, some of them no doubt 'borrowed', would be bought and sold down there. It was very different from Sex. While they had Nureyev shopping there, Acme would have people like Nick Lowe."

Singer/songwriter and producer Lowe would later make his name via collaborations with the likes of Elvis Costello, Johnny Cash and Ry Cooder, but at that time he was leader of rootsy pub rockers Brinsley Schwarz. In late 1973, he transformed his image from denim-clad longhair to glam mod, courtesy of Acme, whose clothes he matched with suits from old-school tailors. "Nick Lowe has turned from plain fun into a real beauty, with a hint of Bowie, even," wrote his one-time flame and performance tightrope walker Hermione Demoriane in her diary on 7 October 1973. Demoriane, who was also briefly a partner of Nick Kent and starred in *Jubilee*, added, "What a sharp dresser! His new, thinner silhouette in a mod suit from Watford, where he found a tailor left over from the era to make him one, makes a good photo for a fan."

Letts' image also blossomed at Acme, and his look was more than a match for many of the customers. He allowed his hair to sprout full-length dreads – a rare sight on the streets of London in 1975 – and wore a leopardskin-print waistcoat and grey flecked trousers with a piece of rope for a belt. "There was no such thing as reggae clothing, so I had more of an attitude. Joe Strummer and Chrissie Hynde lived in my house in Forest Hill at various times, and I got to know Ariana from The Slits, Johnny Rotten and Jah Wobble [demon bass player who was also in Public Image Ltd] through dub."

above Letts and Lee: "It was so cutting edge you couldn't breathe"

Any semblance of cordiality disappeared once the stakes were raised by the emergence of punk. "I used to hang out with Vivienne, go to concerts with her," says Letts, "but then she started to get really rough about the shop and banned me from her's. John used to come down to Acme all the time, not only because he liked our clothes but also it helped to annoy Malcolm, while Sid was always around because he took a shine to Jeanette. The kids who came to us were intelligent enough to know that there is something aesthetically wrong with a punk thing being ready-made and sold for £60. There was a real dichotomy with what [Westwood and McLaren] were doing."

Much later, after Rotten left The Sex Pistols in 1978, Westwood sprayed abusive graffiti targeting the singer over the shop front of Seditionaries. When Letts – who had just spent time filming Rotten on holiday in Jamaica – attempted to shoot footage of the graffiti, he was physically attacked by Westwood. "I literally had to hold her off, physically," he recalls. "She just went wild."

Westwood also ejected Phil Strongman from her shop once he started working at Acme. "I got on quite well with her," says Strongman, who once gave her a book on Durutti. "One day, I was in there talking to her about Joseph Losey films and she started looking at me really curiously. Then she said, 'You work up the road, don't you? I think I'd like you to leave now.'" In Westwood's eyes, alliance with Raynor and Krevine was tantamount to betrayal. "They'd push the envelope, but they're basically completely anal schoolteachers who never understood what us lads were all about," says Raynor. "They looked good, turning up at places in Baader Meinhof T-shirts, whereas we'd turn up with Brighton beach riots on ours. Their thing is very pure – it takes in hardly any influences; it's almost tunnel vision. They didn't look forward, only backward, so all their information came out of history books. Malcolm used to go into public libraries and tear out the pages and put the book back on the shelf in a sort of anarchist statement."

As punk started to break through in the summer of 1976, with bands such as The Clash, Buzzcocks and The Damned catching the wave created by The Sex Pistols, so McLaren and Westwood set about overhauling Sex in order to match the increasingly inflammatory spirit of the times.

In early September, during a trip to Paris for a gig at the opening of a new disco called Le Chalet du Lac, Westwood and Rotten had both worn a new creation: the bondage suit. Tiring of rubberwear, Westwood and McLaren had worked on a design for US marines' fatigues, adding fetish elements such as zips up the back of the calves and thighs to tighten them and another zipper which went from the pubis right around to the back. Fashioned from a sateen material called black Italian, the trousers included buckles on the calves with a belt attached and a towelling bum-flap, while the jacket was zippered and had straps attaching the arms to the body. While McLaren oversaw the campaign to sign The Sex Pistols and handled their increasing recording and touring commitments, Westwood completed a range of designs alongside the bondage suit to

above Jay Strongman, 1977: "God Save The Queen"

129

top Raynor, Krevine and the Acme gang, including (front) Chelsea singer, Gene October

right Bequiffed Phil Strongman in Kensington Market

the US. "The Stray Cats took the whole rockabilly thing nationwide," says Jay Strongman. "The first place they came when they got off the plane from the States was Rock-A-Cha. I remember they brought their suitcases with them into the shop." The group – and in particular singer Brian Setzer – maintained huge pompadour quiffs, and added a punk energy to the basic rockabilly sound. They were soon snapped up by a record company, and their brief run of hits, including 'Rock This Town', and support slots for such acts as The Rolling Stones, helped to transmit the look, as did appearances on such TV shows as *Tiswas* and *Top Of The Pops*.

While the musical tastes of most rockabillies was restricted to the pure and original '50s recordings, others – such as Strongman – were opened up to the hip-hop scene then starting to trickle out of New York, via their fashion connections, while in clubs such as Le Kilt and the Beat Route, DJs with catholic tastes – led by Steve Lewis – were spinning old-school '70s funk alongside appearances by contemporary Brit-funk acts such as Light Of The World. "The first time I became aware of 'Rappers' Delight' by The Sugarhill Gang was when Steve Lewis played it at the Beat Route," says Strongman. "I was living this life, going to Rock-A-Cha, being a hardcore rockabilly, then going out and listening to funk."

The clubs were a melting pot of musical and stylistic genres. Four-on-the-floor funk influenced such acts as Manchester's 23 Skidoo, London's Stimulin (led by fashion journalist Alix Sharkey) and Sheffield's ABC, while jazz-funk fans were turning onto the new romantic look, which is how Spandau Ballet came into being. The short-lived boom in Latin music and salsa rhythm sparked the formation of Modern Romance and Blue Rondo À La Turk, the latter acts dressed to the nines in zoot suits created by the former fashion student Chris Sullivan. The most commercially successful of these was Kid Creole And The Coconuts, authentic Latino New Yorkers who enjoyed hits throughout the summer of 1982.

However, the scene was moving too fast to sustain longevity for a lot of groups. Blue Rondo had been on the cover of *The Face* in April 1981, having played a handful of gigs, and by the time their debut album came out on Virgin in the autumn of the following year, fashion had moved on. "I remember Kid Creole was booked by Jon Savage to appear on Granada TV that August," says Strongman, "and in May they booked two coach-loads of people from the Beat Route to be in the audience, expecting zoot suits and key chains. By the end of the summer, when we went up to Manchester for the programme, everyone was in ripped jeans, leather caps, huge motorcycle boots with the steel caps showing. There were a couple of people really ahead of the time wearing MA1 jackets, but most were wearing motorcycle jackets. It had gone from zoot suits to the Marlon Brando look in the space of about four months."

The adoption of shredded jeans and distressed clothing was labelled hard times, after an article in *The Face* by Robert Elms, and was created as a reaction to the new romantic emphasis on materialism and expensive glamourwear, evinced by the launch of the Camden Palace, hosted by Steve Strange, an attempt to take London nightlife upmarket. Hard Times revolved around clubs such the deliberately down-at-heel Dirtbox, where

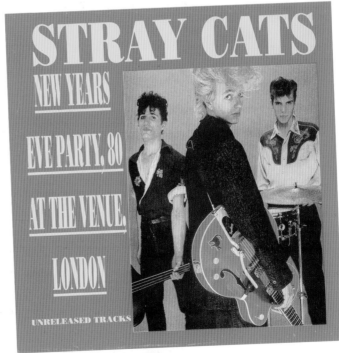

above Madness and The Stray Cats model Johnson's

145

above August Darnell pushes the zoot ethic

right Hard Times: the article which launched a look

Strongman started his DJing career: "Hard times was taking off, and the clothes were perfect for places like the Dirtbox and the warehouse parties which started around then.

The harder edge to dressing up was also expressed in such developments as the sportswear and militaristic clothes made for The Clash in the early '80s by Alex Michon. She had worked with the band throughout the punk era, and was drafted back into the fold to produce the sleeveless jackets and hard-wearing trousers in man-made fabrics worn on the cover of 1982's *Combat Rock*.

Meanwhile, Lloyd Johnson's Rock 'n' Roll Suicide range of late 1981 mixed biker and fighter-pilot imagery with Japanese prints. This included such items as deliberately worn leather jackets with a skullface "Jive Pilot" emblazoned on the back (at £120), while his stark red-and-white rising-sun print appeared on dresses, skirts, shirts and bandannas, and were worn by such artists as Siouxsie Sioux, The Pretenders and Billy Idol. Rock 'n' Roll Suicide is a fine example of the mix-and-match tenor of the post-punk years: everything was up for grabs, and after a hesitant start, the new wave of artists, designers and shop-owners made a concerted effort to turn up forgotten details from the past and to present them in a contemporary style.

None, however, could rival (at least in creative if not financial terms) Vivienne Westwood in her ability to simultaneously shock, arouse and stimulate.

In the wake of The Sex Pistols' catastrophes and the muted reaction to the film of the band's career, *The Great Rock 'n' Roll Swindle*, Malcolm McLaren had fled to Paris, where he claims to have researched music for porn soundtracks. This departure allowed Westwood to reflect on the fact that it was her skill and resourcefulness which had made the major contribution to fashion, a fact which McLaren later acknowledged. "What I probably do for Vivienne is bring her the outside world," he told *The Face*. "I see what she's got and I push her in a direction. I'm the concept man, but she's the tailor."

The "outside world" that McLaren brought to Westwood towards the end of 1979 proved to be typically bizarre yet ultimately cohesive. He had discovered recordings of the thunderous beat of the Burundi tribesmen during his Parisian research, and had also been struck while sitting in the new branch of McDonald's in Wood Green, north London, by the trend among black youths to sport ghetto blasters, on which they played tapes of music pirated from existing recordings. McLaren had also come across striking images of Apache Indians "in some book I stole from Foyles", while he and Westwood researched the gaudy fabrics and jewellery worn by 18th-century pirates.

According to Jane Mulvagh, his brief on a new clothing range for Westwood was "sun, sea and piracy", and he was given an opportunity when approached by Adam Ant with an offer of £1,000 to restyle him and his group, The Ants. Adam was soon ousted by McLaren, who put the musicians together with a 15-year-old ingénue named Anabella Lwin to form Bow Wow Wow. However, Adam took the image, added braided military wear and a white Geronimo war stripe and used it as the basis for his new version of the group. Within a matter of months, the new Adam And The Ants – with Marco Pirroni as co-songwriter – had hit the charts, mixing the Burundi beat with spaghetti western guitar to great effect.

Meanwhile, Bow Wow Wow wore Westwood's new clothes, which she had researched and developed painstakingly over the course of a year. A serpentine squiggle was repeated on white cotton shirts, blouses and scarves in striking colours, while the necks of T-shirts were scrunched sideways, inspired, apparently, by the way in which the polio-stricken Ian Dury wore his clothes. Pirate trousers were made deliberately baggy and from heavy material, the result of many hours investigating such attire at the National Art Library of the V&A.

Once again, 430 King's Road was closed down for extensive refurbishment, and when it re-opened in 1980 all tangible evidence of punk had disappeared. Financed with money from EMI's advance to Bow Wow Wow, the shop's design was put together by Roger Burton, a partner of Steph Raynor's, who had come up with the post-industrial look at PX. Called World's End, the site now resembled a pirate galleon crossed with the Olde Curiosity Shop. The wooden floorboards sloped and were deliberately warped, and outside a huge 13-hour clock ran crazily backwards. Inside could be found a smaller version of the clock, while the shop's staff – including Derek Dunbar and Simon Barker – dressed in the new range, with Rasta-style hobo hats and strap-laden boots in leather and suede.

Westwood also touted the clothes to the growing club market, setting up a stall on the opening night of Philip Salon's Planets in the West End, and in March 1981 the new range was properly inaugurated with the Pirates catwalk show at Olympia. The models – who sported fake tans, gold-tipped nipples and braided hair or mohicans – wore Walkmans and capered on the catwalk, while the hall was decorated with World's End wrapping paper. McLaren and Westwood had injected the first real vitality into couture since the Ossie Clark shows of the late '60s and Kenzo's groundbreaking work in the mid '70s.

The response was strong. *Women's Wear Daily* said that Westwood was "the hottest designer of the new look", and the designer finally began to receive the approval of the fashion establishment. British *Vogue* ran a four-page article on Pirates, and Bloomingdales and Macy's placed orders, albeit for small amounts of the safer lines. Then the V&A ordered a custom-made Westwood outfit for its permanent collection.

Westwood followed up on this success with the Savage collection, which debuted at Olympia in October 1981 and in which the Third World – from Peru and pre-European America to Africa and Aztec – clashed with such contemporary streetwear imagery as the three stripes found on Adidas footwear. The Savage brochure boasted that the clothes were put together "to arouse those instinctive creation rites and work out the taboos that befell us".

In March 1982 the Buffalo range was unveiled in Paris, and this sealed Westwood's reputation. Although over-large and extremely unconventional, the clothes were exquisitely cut and arranged to match the urban wildness and scratching on McLaren's debut single, 'Buffalo Girls'. He contributed superb touches, such as the black kohl stripe smudged across the models' eyes (lifted from *Blade Runner*) and hats with peep-holes cut into them (inspired by *The Elephant Man*), while thick sheepskin coats and jackets were complemented by tall Appalachian hats and rag-like scarves.

Thus began Westwood's new life as a fully-fledged designer, while McLaren's role revolved around ideas and music. When Bow Wow Wow flopped, McLaren continued to display his uncanny ability to pick up on developments in youth culture by recording and mixing together African rhythms with the new hip-hop beats, courtesy of New York's World Supreme Team. These would later appear on his 1983 album, *Duck Rock*, by which time his collaboration with Westwood had ended, as had their personal relationship.

The success of the Buffalo range resulted in the decision to create a new shop, for the first time away from 430 King's Road. Given the brief "mud, Peruvian women and scratch music", Roger Burton set to work on premises in St Christopher's Place, just off Oxford Street, which opened with the name Nostalgia Of Mud in the early summer of 1982, the name a phrase for slumming attributed to writer Tom Wolfe's phrase "*nostalgie de la boue*". Burton created a deliberately collapsed floor, which opened onto a Third World basement decorated with bare scaffolding, an often non-functioning fountain of bubbling mud and caves in which skeletons and fake jewels were embedded. Camouflage tarpaulins were hung from the ceiling and over the entrance, which bore a map of the world, apparently made out of mud. The local trading association was not amused by the design, the clientèle it attracted nor the antics of the exuberantly dressed staff. It swiftly embarked on an ultimately successful campaign to close down the shop.

Westwood went out of her way to stress that the store would not have a direct connection to McLaren's musical projects. "I don't want Bow Wow Wow to have any connection with me any more," she told Chris Salewicz of *The Face*. "I hate them. Malcolm helps design the clothes, and he's involved with them, and I wish he weren't. I wouldn't mind if they were just a mediocre band using their own mediocre ideas. But a mediocre band wasting good ideas is untruthful to me – they just can't carry it. I don't think people want dummies for heroes – they want someone that's true."

So now the lines were drawn: Westwood was in the throes of an unprecedented creative surge, while McLaren was totally immersed in the music business. Her incredible run continued with successive collections: the distressed look of the Hobo-Punkature line received rave reviews in October 1982, while the following year's Witches range took its inspiration from the street and sportswear, and promoted fluorescent colours, the tube skirt (which became a high-street staple) and over-sized trainers. It also incorporated artwork from graffiti supremo Keith Haring.

Financially, however, the business was faltering, and both World's End

and Nostalgia Of Mud began to suffer. Drug addiction among the staff became rife, and there are stories that clothes were sold off cheaply in exchange for ready cash to feed those addictions. Then World's End was closed for at least a year after the bills mounted up and gas and electricity were cut off. In 1984, Westwood shut up shop, having been declared insolvent.

Throughout the succeeding years, Westwood demonstrated a consistent ability to lead fashion, but with scant acknowledgement from the fashion establishment. The mini-crini, the rocking-horse platforms, the puffball skirt – all of these creations undercut the argument that her best work was produced in tandem with McLaren. Throughout, she remained stoutly left field, unable and unwilling to harness her considerable talents to the caprices of the mainstream marketplace. As a result, her finances were often precarious, and there were a series of broken business partnerships.

In 1996, Westwood received a cruel blow when she lost out to John Galliano for the post of design director for Christian Dior, an irony made bitter by the fact that Galliano is one of many who owe her a huge debt – his graduate shows of 1983 were undeniably influenced by Pirates and Buffalo. Galliano's job at Givenchy was taken by another designer who has followed Westwood's iconoclastic path: Alexander McQueen.

These days, her design relationship with husband Andreas Kronthaler has been seen by some – not least by biographer Jane Mulvagh – to have damaged her work, but at least she is receiving the financial recognition so long her due. Financially restructured, her companies, and the designs which sell under the Red and Gold labels, continue to thrive, with total turnover estimated in excess of £20 million per year. With a shop in a prime Mayfair location, Westwood still resides in the south London neighbourhood of Clapham, but now in a fine Georgian terrace rather than the cramped council flat in which she brought up her children and designed some of the most ambitious and outrageous fashion ideas ever realised.

430 King's Road is still World's End, and the clock on the front still whirs forever backwards. Although much posher these days, the area has again become a fashion desert, with high rents forcing out many retailers in favour of mobile-phone emporia and coffee franchises. In 2001, Westwood will celebrate 30 years in the store.

McLaren, meanwhile, is a familiar media figure, his profile raised by his anarchic campaign for the role of Mayor of London, which was based on the sound argument that the position should go to somebody who had contributed to the cultural life of the city, since it has no political teeth. During the electoral race, *The Independent's* columnist Miles Kington described him as "the first honest, decent man to show his colours". Since his withdrawal from the election, McLaren has appeared as an advertising ambassador for Virgin Atlantic and has also been working on his autobiography, which will be published in autumn 2001.

left Vivienne Westwood: "I don't think people want dummies for heroes – they want someone who's true"

149

12 "We're In A Wonderful World Where Everything Goes"

As the '80s progressed, the changes in fashion and music occurred at an increasingly furious pace, revitalised by mainly black genres, specifically the new hip-hop, rap and house and the revival of obscure '60s and '70s funk and soul, labelled rare groove. The rapidity of turnover in looks and styles was also stimulated by the demands of the baby-boomers enjoying the material benefits of the "me" decade. New romantics were as quickly outdated as they had once been cutting-edge, supplanted by the emerging power look which dominated the mid '80s, with its combination of satisfyingly retro and altogether more contemporary and hard-edged flourishes. Fashion became the new rock 'n' roll as particular designers and labels became associated directly with individual performers. By the end of the decade, Pam Hogg, Jean Paul Gaultier and the duo Bernstock Spiers had all made records.

Among the cognoscenti, elements of hip-hop style – baseball caps, Kangol hats, T-shirts, trainers and tracksuits – became the clothes to wear, not at gigs, as rock was consumed by large halls and stadia, but in the clubs which boomed across the UK and in the urban centres of the US.

For some, the decade was the logical conclusion of futurism and the '40s look investigated during the glam and post-punk eras. "The '80s was probably the most outrageous and glamorous fashion period ever," says designer Antony Price. "Think about all those skirts – all short, of course, but the way they got more and more elaborate as the years went by, and the hairdos and the make-up. It was at a Marie Antoinette level by the end."

Price should know. A certain amount of responsibility for the obsession with style during the decade can be placed on his broad shoulders, and he willingly accepts this. "The look I did in the early '70s for Bryan [Ferry] was actually the '80s," he says. "Those slim suits I made for him became one of the trademarks of the era."

Operating out of his shop in the King's Road, which traded under his own name after a two-year spell as Plaza, Price's clothes for both men and women became indelibly associated with the power look and were, after some hesitation, much sought after by rising pop stars who had fallen under the influence of Ferry and Roxy Music during their teens. "At one point, nobody dared buy one of those suits because they didn't want to look like they were directly copying Bryan, because it was so much his trademark," says Price. "Then people like the Duran Durans stopped hovering and went, 'Oh, what the fuck. If he thinks we've copied him, tough.' My generation would wait for people to die before we ripped them off, but this generation? Forget it, honey. If it sells, they'll take it. All those

ethics have gone to the wall completely. There's none of that shit. The only failure is financial failure."

This materialistic worldview was created during the Thatcherite period, when the functional glam offered by the likes of Price was perfect for the power lunch or the private party. Price originally opened Plaza at 341 King's Road under the banner Clothes For Studs And Starlets, a store which featured single-buttoned, broad-shouldered jackets and suits, small-collared shirts and skinny ties. These were complemented by a range of sexy, sophisticated evening wear for women, including a black satin zippered Heroine dress at £75 and a pearlised, black-lace-over-purple-lamé Siren dress (after the one worn by Jerry Hall on the cover of Roxy's fifth album) at £175.

By the time the shop had changed its name to Antony Price, it's interior was so minimalist that there were no clothes on display. Instead, segments were placed on boards with sketches of the individual designs and samples of materials used. Customers chose the garments, which were then made to measure. "People didn't know whether it was a betting shop or a porn place," Price laughs. "The clothes were there but there was just one of each design on display. I didn't want clutter and boxes of crap around, and also I didn't want things nicked, so they were nailed to boards, like a shoe shop or somewhere that sells spanners. It looked like an art gallery, but you ordered your size and it was brought upstairs."

"More hostile than reticent, it deliberately turns an anonymous face to the street," said Vogue at the time. "The façade is impenetrable in dark-blue glass. Computer graphics and a slide box showing enigmatic photographs of the shop's wares offer the only clues to what goes on within." Vogue also quotes Price in confrontational mode: "'This isn't Marks & Spencer, and we don't want those kind of people in here. It's a word-of-mouth thing. I want to bring in the people who have the nerve to push through. No one else will like the clothes, anyway.'" Nevertheless, Price was quickly adopted by artists such as Ultravox, Simple Minds and Duran Duran, none of whom balked at the shop's high prices. Shirts, for example, were £50 each.

Price believes that the menswear boom of the '80s was directly tied to music. "Mary Quant and Twiggy hasn't happened yet," he told a trade newspaper, in reference to two of the leading public faces who triggered the development of womenswear in the '60s. "With Lloyd [Johnson of Johnson's, also in the Kings Road] and myself down here, it's starting. It's all bound up in the rock business, which has changed the menswear

opposite Sixties revival outlet Sign Of The Times, Soho, London, 1988

151

top Bryan Ferry and four-legged friend:
"That look was so much his trademark"

right Antony Price: "It's all bound up in
the rock business"

In Soho, a collective of new designers had formed around Demob, a shop opened on Beak Street by John Baker, who had previously run Axiom. Among those involved was club-runner and Blue Rondo leader Chris Sullivan. The store interior evoked the '40s and '50s by maintaining many of the fittings left by the previous long-term occupant, a fishmonger, but added a hair salon and soda fountain.

The second Demob outlet was opened in St James' Street in 1983, and this branch concentrated on menswear while the original shop turned over to women's fashion. By this time, the company's raft of designers included the innovatory Willy Brown. He had contributed to the starker side of the new romantic movement with his Classics Nouveau outlet, but proceeded to lead the pack with a coherent range of cotton utility clothes. In 1984, Brown's 1916 dress cost £49 at Demob while striped caps were £8 and shirt/jackets were £44.

Brown also launched the XLNT brand, inspired by the art-deco logo of a car factory in Clapham Old Town, south London. This area was later to become the inspiration for his own shop, Willy Brown's Old Town, where he sold traditional shaped trousers, T-shirts and zippered cardigans. The most successful line to bear the XLNT brand was a hooded anorak featuring a checkered strip taken from the classic design of New York yellow cabs, a

design which received the ultimate in fashion flattery when it was ripped off and imitated around the world. As Brown and the other designers went their separate ways, Demob faltered after complaints about the regular parties held at the premises and investigations by the police into allegations of drug usage.

A designer who became deeply associated with the smarter end of '80s style was Paul Smith, a Nottingham-born entrepreneur who opened his first London store in Floral Street, Covent Garden, at the turn of the decade. Suits in such cloths as Prince of Wales check were complemented by a full range of accessories, including Filofaxes, Braun clocks, fountain pens, belts and even works of art, and his business took off with the patronage of David Bowie, Mick Jagger and Bryan Ferry.

By the mid '80s, Smith had launched his business in Japan, and was turning over £2 million a year. "Never think you're a star," he told *The Face*. "In the fashion game, you're only as good as today or tomorrow. As soon as you think you've made it, *whoosh!* Everybody passes you by." Today, Smith continues to operate his global business, its success undoubtedly predicated on such northern pragmatism.

Meanwhile, the Italian Anglophile Elio Fiorucci, who had employed graffiti artist Keith Haring to decorate the interior of his flagship store in

above Demob, Soho, 1984 – formed around a collective of designers

157

Milan, took the decision to rationalise his UK business into a single King's Road store in 1983 after selling his branded goods through a number of outlets. "Fiorucci was really big with us jazz-funkers," says Jenny Ross, a member of local tribe the Sussex Soul System, who would travel up to the company's original London store in Knightsbridge from her home in Sussex to buy Fiorucci jeans to wear at weekenders in resorts such as Caistor. "We were into things like their thin, printed belts, and especially the straight-legged jeans, which were really expensive for the time – around £25 – but fantastic quality."

With clothing contributions from British designers such as Vivienne Westwood and Terry Jones, Fiorucci's stunning shop in the King's Road featured a split-level interior, put together by design team Memphis, which provided a wide-open space to showcase the playful range around a central staircase. This included entire lines in Day-Glo colours, which sold out almost immediately.

An outlet which fought an ultimately successful battle to reassert traditional tailoring values in the '80s was Powell & Co, at 11 Archer Street, in the heart of Soho. "I can remember when Perry Haines brought Duran Duran in when I was working at Robot. I'd never seen such a naff bunch of guys in my life," grins Powell, still in Soho but now in the headquarters of his bespoke tailoring business, high above Brewer Street, surrounded by books and prints of classic suits. "They're not the only ones, though. George Michael must cringe when he looks at some of his pictures from the '80s. He looked so bad. But, mind you, most people did. For the best demonstration of how naff rock 'n' roll people are, look at tapes of the Live Aid concert from 1985. All that long hair chopped off at the sides. Look at Bono! Now he's this cool guy with the shades and the nice suits."

At least as instructive as Live Aid was its successor, Fashion Aid, a charity gala event held at the Albert Hall in November 1985 which provided a formal (if uneasy) bridge between the worlds of music and fashion in support of Sir Bob Geldof's campaign to end world famine. The traditional contingent were represented by Jean Muir, Bruce Oldfield, Zandra Rhodes and Emanuel, and there were are some great touches from the likes of Joseph Ettedgui and Issey Miyake, although some, such as Calvin Klein, revealed themselves to be woefully out of touch by relying on hackneyed versions of the clothes worn by movie icons of the '30s and '40s. Meanwhile, Giorgio Armani's sedate collection that was on display at Fashion Aid was introduced by the unusual combination of actress Anjelica Huston and soon-to-be-ex-member of Wham! Andrew Ridgeley.

Newer talents such as Jasper Conran utilised the cartoonesque qualities of Madness to model his range of clothes in startling primal colours, while Eurythmics' Dave Stewart and Annie Lennox introduced designer Katharine Hamnett by claiming that she was "the woman who had changed everyone's view of the relationship between fashion and causes by putting her heart on her sleeve and her views on everyone's chests".

In 1984, Hamnett had struck upon the idea of using the blank canvas of the over-large white T-shirts to make simplistic political statements,

such as "Choose Life!" and "No Nukes". In that same year, her contribution to the Venice Carnivale was a model dressed as an industrial smokestack labelled "Pollution" to show the effects on the environment of toxic waste.

Hamnett had gained tabloid notoriety by wearing a T-shirt bearing the anti-nuclear weapons message "63% Don't Want Pershing!" to a reception at 10 Downing Street, where she was photographed alongside Margaret Thatcher, and this was increased when she came up with the phrase "Frankie Say No!" to tie in with the Frankie Goes To Hollywood hit 'Two Tribes'. When this anti-war statement was bootlegged around the world, Frankie's name was made and Hamnett's reputation sealed, although it should be noted that she had also come up with slogan T-shirts for the Wham! single 'Wake Me Up Before You Go-Go' and the official Live Aid slogan, "Let's Save The World".

Two very different designers were given prominence at Fashion Aid, and this underlines the contribution that they were making to musical style at the time. Scott Crolla was known for his tapestry waistcoats and printed Nehru jackets at his store at 35 Dover Street, and clients such as Spandau Ballet's Martin Kemp, Patsy Kensit, Richard Jobson, Steve Strange and even veteran DJ Alan Freeman took to the stage modelling his gaudy clothes. In as early as 1983, designer Stephen Linard had hailed Crolla's as being "the only menswear shop in London offering something new...a perfect blend of adventurous tailoring and witty fabrics". Although now forgotten amid the blaze of publicity behind Jean Paul Gaultier's work with Madonna and his skirts for men, the French designer's first ranges available in London via Bazaar were clothes very much in the Crolla vein: striped silk smoking jackets, brightly-checked waistcoats and gaberdine trousers, as worn by Frankie Goes To Hollywood's Paul Rutherford and Holly Johnson.

opposite Paul Smith: "In the fashion game, you're only as good as today or tomorrow"

above Paul Smith (l): "Never think you're a star"

above Ringo Starr, Roger Waters and
Pete Townshend: "Look at how naff rock
stars looked in the '80s"

160

British invasion. While the company's catwalk shows challenged convention by using elderly people and babies, bad business dealings and the lack of faith demonstrated by the mainstream industry in Body Map's more avant-garde leanings were to prove its undoing. The company eventually collapsed in financial ruin.

However, the Body Map team are among the very few who escaped Fashion Aid with their dignity intact, which was very indicative of the times, as Mark Powell notes: "Pop stars were all really naff."

The ever-ebullient Powell's career as a menswear obsessive started when he acquired his first pair of Levi's as a six-year-old in Romford, Essex. Having moved through the various youth tribes, from pre-pubescent suedehead to rockabilly via soul boy, he worked at Italian import shop Washington Tremlett and '50s shoe and suit specialist Robot before opening Powell and Co in 1984, after coming across a warehouse full of original '40s and '50s clothes in Stoke Newington. "By that time, I had gotten into the original 1952 Teddy boy look, very neo-Edwardian. I started to develop it by research and made it more purist, with a four-button suit; shirt with starched, detachable, high, rounded collar; big knotted tie with pearl stick pin; waistcoat; and Balmoral boots, or spats when I could find them. That later became Vic Reeves' look, and it wasn't authentic, more what you might see on Peter Cushing in a Hammer film."

Among Powell's customers in Archer Street were Bryan Ferry, David Bowie and the members of Sade, as well as friends such as Chris Sullivan. Powell soon started to play around with certain images from the past, including a Regency dandy look in velvet and what he describes as "the Ronnie and Reggie gangster thing". He made his mark with such geezer chic a decade later, as evident in the movie *Lock, Stock And Two Smoking Barrels*, but there wasn't much place in the dominant club culture at that time for dandies in tight three-piece suits.

He also contributed clothing to Julien Temple's 1985 cinematic débâcle *Absolute Beginners*, based on Colin MacInnes' '50s Soho teen novel, which starred Patsy Kensit (then leading wannabe pop act Eighth Wonder) and featured appearances from David Bowie and Sade and many other mid-'80s fashion and music players. However, poor writing and editing, combined with the lack of a charismatic male lead, resulted in an expensive flop. At this distance it isn't without its charms, according to Powell: "Although it's a terrible film, and badly put together, there are some elements which are really good and sum up London at the time."

Absolute Beginners also details the pseudo-beatnik and jazz style still being sported by the first wave of club movers and shakers, but their days were numbered as a fresh generation of suburban kids swept into the West End, creating around them the rare groove scene and sowing the seeds for the late-'80s explosion of club culture.

In 1985, Tony Farsides was travelling into the West End from his parents' home in the outer north London suburb of Mill Hill, drawn to the clubs of Soho. "We were a new crowd coming into the West End, who were a bit younger than that older club lot," says Farsides, now a writer. "We

Meanwhile, back at Fashion Aid, the intricate designs and clubwear of Body Map's Stevie Stewart and David Holah drew a performance from vocalist Helen Terry, and among the models cavorting to the electro dance track 'After The Rainbow' was her startlingly quiffed Culture Club colleague Boy George.

Body Map had won the Most Innovative Designer Of The Year award in 1983, and had made its mark with a collection entitled Querelle Meets Olive Oyl, which mixed homo-eroticism with swirls and sportswear, drawing £100,000 in orders. With a coterie which included the contemporary dancer Michael Clarke and film-maker John Maybury, they soon outgrew their Camden Market beginnings and by 1985 were employing a staff of 20, although Stewart and Holah had hedged their bets by maintaining a utility range at Kensington Market, attracting in the process such pop stars as Chrissie Hynde while they courted the international fashion business.

But in the middle of the decade, US trade magazine *The Daily News Record* wondered whether Body Map was "an outrageous pretension or a pretentious outrage", underlining a withdrawal of support for the so-called

on its head with his bizarre appearance.

Bowery's designs, which had been picked up early on by New York entrepreneur Suzanne Bartsch, had included such elements as velvet robes and velour tops matched with fetishistic adornments such as nose, eyebrow and nipple piercings. His friends and models, Trojan (who died of a drug overdose in 1987) and David, also took to dyeing their faces and upper torsos in vidvid reds and blues. "It's only a small scene at the moment, but other designers like Westwood and Body Map are picking up on it," he boasted in 1984. "I'm certain my look will catch on."

Bowery also ran his own club, the outrageous Taboo, which was backed by entrepreneur Tony Gordon and provided the '80s meeting place for fashionistas and musicians, including Body Map, John Galliano, John Richmond of Richmond Cornejo (who had clothed acts such as ABC and later created an '80s staple with his range of shirts featuring the word "Destroy" printed down the sleeves), Paul Bernstock of Bernstock Spiers and Jasper Conran. Musician regulars included Spandau Ballet, Frankie Goes To Hollywood, Paul Young, ABC and, inevitably, Boy George, who said at the time, "For me, Leigh Bowery is Taboo. Without him, it would be another sweaty run-down Jewish disco."

By 1988, Bowery had moved on from his trademark ink-spilled egghead look into entirely new territory. "He was wearing this fucking twisted outfit," says George. "One of his eyes was plastered down. On his head was this thing with spikes sticking up and his the mouth was all to one side. He had these checkered breasts with his arse out, and all these people were on ecstasy. This thing appeared, and it really freaked everyone out. It was so out there people didn't know what to say."

George describes the Australian-born Bowery (who went on to become the muse for painter Lucien Freud and died in 1996) as one of the most important style influences of the last two decades. "I think Leigh had watched from afar, and when he arrived in London he just decided to take things further. One of the things I liked about him was the fact that he didn't have hang-ups about his body. I was at the Fridge one night and he was in this kind of puffball headdress with a push-up bra, a vagina wig and these boots, but nothing else. He was dancing around and I can remember looking at him and thinking, 'That's so fucking brave to come out in public with his arse out – and a big arse at that!' What was unusual about Leigh was that he used clothes and make-up to make a point, whereas we all use them to disguise our defects."

Bowery was all about driving the made-up finery and shock value of the early new romantics that he had read about while still in Melbourne in the early '80s to a logical conclusion, although not many followed the trail he blazed. Instead, most clubbers opted for the easy and safe option of streetwear, much of it influnced by the beach lifestyle.

Jane Bussman points out that pioneering beachwear labels such as Gotcha, Quiksilver and Hot Tuna were all eclipsed by Stussy, founded by self-confessed Californian beach bum Shawn Stussy. His striking T-shirts and small matching ranges of shorts and hats were originally sold

above Leigh Bowery: "He was wearing this fucking twisted outfit"

through American Classics in the UK before transferring to one of the first streetwear vendors, EndZone, in Newburgh Street. "Stussy really made sense to me in the way they presented themselves through advertising, using skateboarding and hip-hop imagery," says Fraser Cooke. "It was very B-Boy-ish. This was the first time that anyone had done those items of clothing properly. There was no such thing as streetwear until they came along."

Michael Koppelman first met Stussy through a mutual friend, and was struck by how the designer's clothes were out of sync with what was going on. "There was this whole scene revolving around places like the Café de Paris and the Criterion, and Shawn was coming up with something different, tracksuits and reggae-style or surf-style T-shirts. His stuff was completely revolutionary."

Eventually, EndZone relinquished the franchise, and following the financial crash of 1988 Koppelman was in a position to start handling distribution. "I got asked to leave my job in the City, basically, and got a year's money," he says. "I already knew Shawn, and he asked me to go with a load of my friends to Japan to DJ over there. When I came back, I decided to do fashion stuff."

Koppelman believes that Stussy's secret is that the brand has maintained credibility, even though its founder has now left the business to concentrate on the beach life in California and Hawaii. "We were and are in love with that company. Because I had been working for big companies, I was very anti them. I liked the idea of it being a small thing and selling to like-minded people. At that time, if you saw someone wearing that stuff, you just knew they were of a like mind.

"It's difficult to say exactly what is so special about Stussy. It's a graphics-led company, and there are lots of others who have tried but none have achieved it. The clothes are comfortable, and you can wear them on the beach, in the sports hall, to a club or a wedding. Now it really annoys me when I see high fashion brands making similar stuff and selling it really expensively and people thinking that's really credible. Stussy was the first company to make casual American sportswear, and it still has that innocence and purity. It was one of the first clothing brands for home boys and skaters, who have been behind so much innovation and energy in clothing."

Stussy's success prompted a slew of imitators, providing business for the brand import shops which followed in the wake of shops such as Utopia and EndZone. Just around the corner from EndZone, in Litchfield Street, Keith Haring print T-shirts and all manner of "one-stop globalism" was supplied by World, owned by the constantly clubbing couple Michael and Gerlinda Kostiff, who were said to turn up at Shoom in full Tibetan national dress, and who were also very close to Vivienne Westwood. They later launched the night club Kinky Gerlinky, but at World they sold long-sleeved T-shirts printed with motor-racing sponsors' logos, wool caps with the Playboy bunny, bum bags, dolls, dresses and miniature roller-skates.

World in turn inspired stores such as Bond in Newburgh Street, run by "designer wide boys" Kevin Reid and Adrian Garrett, who stocked lines ranging from John Smedley knitwear to Hanes T-shirts before going all out for streetwear. The streetwear phenomenon took off with Passenger, in Brewer Street, and fishermen's hats, logo T-shirts, pastel-coloured sweatshirts and the clothes and jeans made by such companies such as Manchester's Joe Bloggs became the uniform of the dance-influenced baggy groups, led by The Stone Roses and The Happy Mondays.

"You had all these clothes coming through at the same time as people were into dressing down for clubs," says Cooke, who became a buyer for Passenger's owner, Sean Turpin, bringing over such desirable labels as Carrhart and Adidas. "It was perfect, really. I remember Office shoes had just opened, and they steamed in at a trade fair in Atlanta, ordering all these shell-toe trainers from Adidas. It hadn't gone massive then, and we didn't have the faith to think it would go that big, but it did. Subsequently, that was what every student was wearing."

Cooke later fell out with Turpin, and after a brief return to hairdressing he pitched up at Black Market, working alongside Tony Farsides in 1989. This was the height of orbital raves, when such hip record shops were hives for ticket-buyers eager to find a field within the radius of the M25 in which to take drugs and cavort to house. "We were in the back selling £25 tickets for events like Sunrise, and the shop was making a fortune," says Cooke. "I was a bit of a Soho trendy at the time, going to places like Fred's and the Café de Paris, so I didn't really like the idea of hanging out with a load of E'd-up Millwall supporters.

"Initially, acid house was pretty good – there was this mental explosion like nothing we'd ever seen, mainly because it had nothing to do with the media dictating it – but then the music became really tacky, and it became all about the drugs. I felt like house had ruined clubbing, turning it into this nightmare prospect. It was naffness personified."

However, in *Once In A Lifetime*, DJ Terry Farley is quoted as making an important point about the apparent anonymity of acid house style: "'I hear people say that it didn't matter what you wore in those days – that's absolute bollocks. You might have been wearing dungarees, but it had to be the right dungarees, and you knew that they were.'"

One shop which became associated with acid house but managed to maintain credibility all the while, appealing to the hippest clubbers and squealing pop fans alike, was Red Or Dead, which had been founded as a market stall in Camden Town in the early '80s by Wayne Hemingway, the son of a native American pugilist called Billy Two Rivers, who had first met his mother in Morecambe, Lancashire.

"I was always into music and fashion, like Barry Manilow," snorts the deadpan Hemingway in his smart suburban mansion in northwest London. "My mum had me in her early 20s, and she was obsessed with music. She also used to make clothes, and when I was around three or four she used to dress me up, one week as a mod, the next week as a rude boy. I look like a right little twat in the pictures, and I'd never do it with my kids, but looking back it's really funny. I was like this little toy, a little music fashion accessory. She was living out her dress sense through me, and it became a

we viewed clothes as artists," says Karie. "You'd look at each collection as an album, and there needed to be a hit single. You need the single to market the album, and vice versa. And the label, whether it's X-Large or Toca, has to be a bit of a pop star, at least [enough] to attract the magazines, because then you get a name. Everything we sell has kind of a feeling of being marketed; that's why we're less a fashion shop as a fashionable shop."

Brooks admits that Shop will often be swayed by the characters behind the labels rather than by the clothes themselves. "You become a bit fascinated by a personality, as opposed to whether or not what they're doing is particularly fashionable. Like Kim Gordon doing X-Girl – we loved that whole thing. We also decided that we were going to love the clothes before we'd probably even seen them."

The launch of the Shopgirl brand in 2000 was also musically informed. "The name is kind of a homage to X-Girl," says Karie, "but it also has a derogatory feel to it, labelling someone as a merely a sales assistant. But [Garbage singer] Shirley Manson was a sales assistant in Miss Selfridge, and she always thought, 'I'm going to make it,' and we always thought that was great. It's a bit of the underdog, a bit 'Poor cow, you're going to make it after all, despite what people think.'"

The decision to call the new group Shopgirl also echoes the links between Sex and The Sex Pistols. "It's a vehicle for the band to promote itself," says Karie. "We might as well exploit the collision between pop and fashion, like Calvin Klein when he employs Kim Gordon and Foxy Brown to model his clothes in ads. If you get it right on that level, it's free advertising. And why shouldn't we? Madonna's a right-on artist who's respected for her determination, but she will still model for Donatella Versace for $100,000."

A recent success for Shop has been its hook-up with traditional undergarment manufacturer Damart. This line of clothing, produced under the Shopgirl brand, featured skimpy lace-edged tops and knickers which were eagerly snapped up by performers such as Geri Halliwell. Her erstwhile Spice Girls colleague Melanie B acquired a Dead In England "Too Fast To Live Too Young To Die" T-shirt via her stylist from Shop. "There were pictures of her wearing it in *Hello*," gasps Karie. "She cropped it to show her belly-button piercing. It's so weird that she'd be wearing that anyway, because she's so not punk. It was really inappropriate and really wrong, but it just shows the power of stylists."

The fact that The Spice Girls straddled the '90s as style icons speaks volumes about pop fashion, from the calculated outrage of Halliwell's revealing Union-Jack dress at the 1996 Brit Awards to Mel B's appearances on the catwalks during London Fashion Week. "There was something genius about The Spice Girls, though," says Boy George. "They had the cheap, council-estate appeal that worked very well for the times." That was at the launch, however, when their images produced branded clothes to identify with each member – tracksuits for Sporty and junglist wear for Scary. By the launch of their reunion album, *Forever*, in autumn 2000, the links with high fashion were firmly established; in mass-market lads' mags

left "You're going to make it, despite what people think"

below The Spice Girls: "They had cheap, council-estate appeal which worked for the times"

shirts, as well as their X-Large label. Shop has also stocked Malcolm McLaren's Dead In England label, which revived some of the classic Sex T-shirts, and for a short period it also sold classic ranges from Fiorucci. One of its designers is Stevie Stewart, the founder of Body Map.

Karie first encountered Brooks in Fred's, the late-'80s Soho media haunt, where he was DJing while she was performing some of her songs. "We've always had a musical bond," says Max in Shop's offices, which overlook the rooftops and neon signs of Soho. The pair also worked in a Covent Garden boutique called Venus, selling second-hand clothes as well as the occasional John Galliano and Vivienne Westwood line. In 1995, they opened Shop, having previously operated an outlet within the Laundry, where they sold the "Rock Star" T-shirt produced by Keith Richards' ex Anita Pallenberg, as well as clothes designed by pre-eminent '80s stylist Judy Blame. "We set Shop up along the lines of the rock business in that

top right "There was something genius about The Spice Girls"

middle DJ Sean Rowley models New Lad style for Oasis

bottom Oasis and Creation Records' Alan McGee in Britpop finery

above Noel Gallagher in Burro fur jacket

such as British *Esquire*, the quartet were dressed to the nines in Missoni, DKNY, Ralph Lauren, Helmut Lang and Gucci.

At least The Spice Girls went for glamour, which cannot be said of the other huge British act of the '90s, Oasis. While frontman Liam Gallagher commands an undeniable cool, the band's clothes were imitated by legions of fans happy to settle for the new lad uniform of expensive if anonymous-looking jeans, checked button-down Ben Sherman shirts (a nod to the casual/mod roots of Britpop but always worn outside the jeans), anoraks and brand-name trainers, desert boots or Gucci loafers.

At Shop, Brooks and Karie have developed a style which offers the antithesis to new lad, underlined by their licensing deal with Playboy Inc. In the summer of 2000, the store unveiled the first fruits of this partnership when the familiar logo started to appear in sparkling form on T-shirts and as pendants and earrings. "If it's something you can get anywhere, we don't really see much of a point having it," says Karie. "Not that we want to stock weird shit that doesn't sell – there's a fine line between being arty and arsey – but put it this way: we wouldn't sell Diesel. We were approached by Diesel and we were approached by Levi's, but we just don't want to sell that shit. You can get Diesel and Levi's in Selfridges. Why would we want to sell it?"

This exclusive approach extends to companies such as X-Large, controlled by The Beastie Boys, which is supplying particular lines to Shop on a one-off basis. X-Large has outlets itself in the US, with stores which used to run adjacent with X-Girl until Kim Gordon took the decision to wind down the company in 1999. "She originally wanted to do cheap, affordable clothes which girls can get into," says Brooks. "That was a fantastic premise, but she decided to shut it rather than have it continue as a commercial venture without her input."

Among Shop's heroines is Courtney Love, who has worn many of the outlet's clothes. "She's so great because people don't understand her," claims Karie. "When she had that reputation [of being] a heroin addict, the most punk thing she could do was to go glamorous and be on the cover of *Harper's Bazaar*. People don't want her to do that because they want to see her falling around in the gutter. The other pop star who really cuts it is Lil' Kim. She dresses so well and she's really into fashion, going to Versace shows. I love her style. It's so extreme and so fuck-off."

As the '90s progressed, hip-hop style was wrested out of the control of dressed-down gangstas by rising and confrontationally sexy east coast female stars Lil' Kim, Mary J Blige and Foxy Brown, as well as players such as Biggie Smalls and his producer, Sean "Puff Daddy" Combs, projecting their lifestyle of Cristal, Cuban cigars and couture.

As *Vibe* writer Emil Wilbekin points out in his hip-hop fashion overview, *Great Aspirations*, rappers had long been namechecking fashion brands; way back in the '80s, Slick Rick had talked about putting on "my brand new Gucci underwear". Wilbekin also stresses how designers from Isaac Mizrahi to Todd Oldham and Karl Lagerfeld all appropriated elements of black style in their work, particularly gold chains, while

left Patsy Kensit and Liam Gallagher: undeniably cool

below "Lil' Kim is so extreme and fuck off"

another breakthrough came about in 1994 when Ralph Lauren chose Jamaican model Tyson Beckford to promote his preppy Polo brand. Polo, David Chu's Nautica and Tommy Hilfiger, particularly, later became the sportswear brands of choice, along with black-targeted labels such as FUBU (For Us By Us), backed by the multi-national corporation Samsung.

Some acts opted to produce their own streetwear designs. The Wu-Tang Clan launched their own fashion label, Wu-Wear, and Pras of The Fugees had Refugee Gear. Meanwhile, hip-hop record moguls got in on the act – Russell Simmons currently operates the Phat Farm brand and Master P has his own company.

After years spent behind the scenes building his own empire, Bad Boy Entertainment, and amassing a personal fortune estimated at $120 million, Puff Daddy first launched a recording career as a solo artist and then as a self-proclaimed "ghetto fabulous" fashionista. Puffy had modelled for Hilfiger (along with Raekwon, Jodeci and the late Tupac Shakur's girlfriend, Kidada Jones), and witnessed the power wielded by fashion first hand. Wilbekin points out that Hilfiger sweatshirts sold out in New York the day after Snoop Doggy Dogg had appeared on *Saturday Night Live* wearing one.

Such power drew Puffy, as did associations with American *Vogue* editor Anna Wintour and Donatella Versace. He started in the fashion business in 1998, with a range of hip-hop jeans for his Sean John brand, and joined in with the fashion shows in New York in the winter of 2000 with his first fashion collection, for which models wore white fur coats, black leather trousers and millions of dollars' worth of diamonds. "Hey, I'm like a real designer," he told *The Daily Telegraph Magazine*'s Catherine Wilson in April 2000. "I feel like a lot of men's fashion is boring. Sean John is sexy, hip-hop and rock 'n' roll…A lot of times, people just try to say the ghetto is negative. I am talking about the positive things. The soulfulness mixed with the fabulousness. A lot of men feel they have to be so reserved, so cool, it becomes boring."

While it looks unlikely that the next menswear fashion trend will be based on sporting voluminous white fur coats over bare chests strung with diamonds, it is true that conservatism crept back in during the '90s. In menswear, the suit made a major comeback, propelled by bespoke operators such as Mark Powell, who produced clothes for album covers and live performances by the likes of Bryan Ferry, Wet Wet Wet, Take That and The Cranberries. "I really got stuck back into it and did tons of stuff: Madness for a Sekonda advert, the Black Watch tartan suit George Michael wore at the Wembley AIDS concert, jackets and trousers for Dinah Carrol, Siobhan Fahey, even Mel B. She was wearing an orange suit I made for her when she met Prince Charles."

In 1992, Powell started to develop a look which was taken up first by Take That and then by Boyzone and which later became a boy-band staple: suits with full-length coats, usually in darker hues and usually in velvet. He was also first on the block in developing the gangster style which crossed over in the film *Lock, Stock And Two Smoking Barrels*. "I

was keeping a strong element of tradition, the Savile Row thing, in such a way that it becomes fashion," he claims. "That's the reason people come to me. Once they've done all that designer gear, they can't really go anywhere else, so where do they go? A tailor."

During the late '80s, Powell had run a tongue-in-cheek easy-listening night in Soho called Violet's, after the Kray twins' mother. He gave up after a couple of years, but in 1994, as London started to swing again and the British economy boomed, a number of dandies and fancy dressers coalesced around a new easy-listening movement. Clubs such as Cheese, Smashing and Blow-Up celebrated the new financial vigour by playing the smooth sounds of Bacharach and Tony Bennett alongside foreign-movie soundtracks and '60s and '70s library-music albums. But the key venue was Indigo, at Soho drag bar Madame Jo Jo's, a club which continues to this day.

"Around that time, there was nowhere really to go because house music had this grip on the body politic," says Bruce Marcus, who styles himself as Count Indigo. "I'd never been an out-and-out night-clubbing person because I like talking to people, so I decided to set up my own cabaret club, a place where you could dance, eat, watch an act and chat as well. In the first six weeks, the DJs were playing soundtracks and library music between the acts, and then it just took off very, very quickly. All these people came out of the woodwork, and there was this media-invented easy-listening scene."

Marcus was brought up in Northampton and attended a boarding school as a day boy, the only black kid among 400 pupils. Having flirted with two-tone, he developed a mid-century gentleman's look while working at the town's premier second-hand clothing emporium, Scrooge. "There were a lot of goths there, because it was the home of Bauhaus, but I couldn't get into that look. I was into electro groups like DAF and The Gang Of Four, street political music and agit-pop, but I suppose I didn't look like most people listening to that music."

Certainly not. Marcus would wear plus-fours and a herringbone jacket to gigs and clubs. "I've always had this conservative/radical chic thing going on," he says. "There was an element of 'Know thine enemy.' Where I went to school, I got a good education on the dos and don'ts of the landed gentry, and I guess I've always had a love/hate thing about it which was expressed in those clothes, though of course you can go into self-parody, like Chris Eubank."

Having arrived in London to study the history of film, Marcus' interest in vintage clothing was fed by places such as Camden Market, while his musical tastes extended to overtly political artists such as Billy Bragg and Paul Weller. "I was into their theory of popular frontism, that '30s ideal of a creative and cultural life which fits into political objectives," he says. "I just thought they had really bad style, so I wanted to present it properly."

After college and a stint at the British Film Institute, Marcus developed a performance piece based on twelve songs by the US beat poet Jack Hammer, which he premièred at the Edinburgh Festival, and later fronted a band called Clay And The Magnificent. "We were

somewhere between Orange Juice and The Brand New Heavies, if you can see a link. I can't see one, so maybe that's why we weren't signed!"

Then, in late 1994, Indigo opened at Madame Jo Jo's. "On the first night, we had a string quartet playing Astor Piazzola and obscure film music in a classical vein. The DJs were playing soundtracks and easy stuff because it's the best music for dancing to and talking through and it doesn't jar with live performance." Marcus was by this time wearing '60s Italian suits and starting to pick up on '70s style – larger collars, wider ties and flared suits. "It was reminiscent of night-club scenes from *The Persuaders*. Then I started to meet all these people, like Mike Flowers, who had a twelve-piece band in dickie bows which just couldn't find a suitable place to play."

Other new acquaintances included performers such as Jackie Clunes, DJs James and Martin Karminsky and club-runners Martin Green and Paul Tonkin. With attendees including the singer Björk ("I think she used to come because we played Yma Sumac," says Marcus) and Pulp, Indigo rapidly made a name for itself, and also attracted the more mature set, among them actress Barbara Windsor and boss of Virgin, Sir Richard Branson. "We even had those Spice women down," says Marcus. "It was really funny, because they asked the DJ to play disco and he informed them that they were in a lounge/easy club so there was none. Then they sent their bouncer over to have a word. In one way, it did have VIP élan, but I thought it was a bit naff."

There were live performances at Indigo by easy gods such as Tony Bennett and Burt Bacharach, as well as new lounge exponents such as Combustible Edison and French pop fans Baby Birkin. Record companies soon hooked up with figures from the scene to re-evaluate their back catalogues, resulting in releases such as EMI's two *Sound Gallery* volumes, The Kandinskys' *In-Flight Entertainment* and Paul Tonkin's *Blow-Up* series.

In the States, the growth of lounge prompted Capitol Records to release its exhaustive, 18-part *Ultra Lounge* series of albums, while acts such as Japan's Pizzicato Five found a new audience. Marcus also signed a record deal, and during the Christmas of 1995 the scene scored a surprise hit in the charts when The Mike Flowers Pops' version of the Oasis song 'Wonderwall' went to Number Two.

In fashion terms, the lounge look was co-opted by designers such as Gucci, who produced '70s-style clothes in gaudy synthetics. Although easy's novelty value was confirmed by the flash-in-the-pan success of Mike Flowers, the influence of the movement endures, notably in the French disco of acts such as Air and Etienne de Crecy. "If you think about it, Portishead were one of the quintessential '90s acts," points out Marcus. "But they're basically Lalo Schifrin with a sampler."

One of the influences which went into the easy/lounge melting was Tiki music, based on the '50s enjoyment of South Seas and Polynesian culture in the US, which is best manifested in Hawaiian shirts and cocktail bars such as Trader Vics. Lloyd Johnson made a brave attempt to shift Tiki into the mainstream, inspired by repeated trips to the west coast. "I went over

top left Bruce Marcus: "There's always an element of 'know thine enemy'"
left French pop revivalists Baby Birkin revive '60s uncool for the mid-'90s

179

to LA and walked into the Lava Lounge," he recalls, referring to the stunningly designed retro bar which opened on the west coast in 1995. "The Blue Hawaiians [a hip instrumental act] were playing the theme from *Beat Girl*, and I thought I'd died and gone to heaven!"

In response to the hegemony of the personality-free '90s dressed-down look (which constituted multi-pocketed and voluminous combat trousers and zippered fleece jackets), Johnson had already started to produce a range of Rat-Pack wear: shiny sharkskin suits, fancy shirts, gaudy patent leather shoes, rhinestone tie-pins and cufflinks and short-sleeved flyaway-collared shirts adorned with dragons and oriental imagery. Bands such as The Fun Lovin' Criminals adopted the look wholesale. "I did the Vegas stuff because I was sick to death of seeing people dressed like they just walked off a campsite," he says, referring to the look which was dominated by the anorak. "It looks like Milletts with a Stussy label on it. There is a big market for people who want to go out and dress up and have a laugh. I like kitsch, but I decided to make making it wearable and very sophisticated."

Johnson opened a new shop on Portobello Road in the summer of 1998 as a showcase for the Vegas and Tiki looks. Complete with bamboo bars and raffia work, the shop stocked exotica albums by the likes of Arthur Lyman, Les Baxter and Yma Sumac as well as South Seas-style shirts, dresses and shorts. "I wanted to ensure it wasn't a fashion thing," he says. "The Hawaiian and rock 'n' roll shirts were perfect to wear with fatigues. If I was in it for the money, I'd have sold down and fleece jackets, but those shirts had such variety – a cocktail one, a Vegas one and a Tiki one. They go great with Birkenstocks." Many performers agree. Fatboy Slim picked up many items to add to his large collection of loud shirts, while Noel Gallagher opted for the more muted dragon style.

By this time, a swing revival had taken place in the US, powered by such acts as The Cherry Poppin' Daddies and The Brian Setzer Orchestra. Utilised in films such as *Swingers* and played at west coast clubs such as the Derby, in LA, it was a short-lived phenomenon whose fashion appeal was restricted to the US, while the lindy-hop became just another step to be taken up at dance classes in church halls around the UK.

Similarly, Johnson's Tikified outlet in Notting Hill failed to hit commercially. The crowds who teemed around Portobello Road maintained a preference for combat trousers, and were soon buying knocked-off dragon shirts in inferior fabrics from market stalls just a few yards down the road. "I would have liked to see the swing thing take off, because people would have become more aware of shoes rather than trainers," says Johnson mournfully. "Sportswear is just so dull. There's a lot to be done with it, but people don't bother. You could make it more space-age and less like Candice-Marie and Keith from *Nuts In May*."

Having closed his original outlet in Kensington Market after 25 years in mid 1999, Johnson was also forced to shut the Tiki shop in the autumn of that year. After this, outrageous rent increases squeezed him out of his King's Road outlet at the beginning of 2000. Now he is embracing the internet, and has a licensing deal with US clothing distributor BC Ethic.

top right Lloyd Johnson and Jay Strongman in Tiki Heaven, London W11

right Beatnik revival clothes for the '90s

Now there are a number of organisations which have demonstrated strong demand for his Tiki shirts, including marine bases.

Johnson's ability to achieve commercial success without a shop is indicative of the changing circumstances of pop fashion. Some are glad that the period of transition is finally complete. "The '90s was a nightmare, the most dreary period in history," says designer Antony Price, who was absent from the scene for much of the decade. "Thank God it's come to an end! All we had were people walking around in black shifts with two straps and hugely expensive labels. There was no work in those garments at all. All the money that was paid for those clothes went on the advertising, because the companies are so desperate to be successful and don't want to get up people's noses."

IT'S REAL

TOMORROW'S TRUTH TODAY

2000 SPRING/SUMMER EDITION

FREE SPECIAL ISSUE
EXCLUSIVE
THE SHOCKING INSIDE STORY OF A FALLING STAR. DAY BY DAY. MINUTE BY MINUTE.

MEET THE VICTIMS, THE WITNESSES, THE LOVERS, THE FRIENDS, THE NEIGHBOURS. ONLY IN IT'S REAL!

COUNTRY-ROCK STAR JOANNA ATTACKS PREGNANT WOMAN!

Colour pictures inside!

It's true because It's Real!

The dirty country girl plays dirty when denied entry to club

Many secret details!

EXCLUSIVE by **JAMES ROBERTON**

POLISH-BORN COUNTRY-ROCK STAR JOANNA Zychowicz, known as Joanna, who instantly reached number one on the world's country-rock charts with her catchy hit "Dirty Country Girl" last summer, has since had a remarkable career. Her new CD "The Luxury of Dirt" has been climbing the charts rapidly. But everything seems to be falling to pieces. IT'S REAL has the full story. On Wednesday night as Joanna was trying to enter the down town club The Twitty Twit, she was denied entry. "She wasn't properly dressed, she was wearing dirty clothes"...

FULL STORY: Page 3

DID JOANNA HAVE PLASTIC SURGERY PERFORMED ON HER NOSE?

THE FULL INSIDE STORY ON PAGE 24

Joanna and boyfriend Rick abandon terrified witnesses and victims outside the club

THE LUXURY OF DIRT TERROR THE LUXURY OF DIRT TERROR THE LUXURY OF DIRT TERROR